# SELECTED VERSE OF ÉMILE NELLIGAN

## Québec's great lyric poet

### Translated with commentary by

## Ian Allaby

Selected Verse of Émile Nelligan: Québec's great lyric poet
Translated with commentary by Ian Allaby (c) 2023

Subjects: French poetry, Canada, Quebec, Montreal, 19th century, Émile Nelligan, translation, fixed-form poetry, lyrical poetry, Symbolist poetry, Parnassian poetry, Decadent poetry, Catholicism, schizophrenia.

Front cover image: *The Lute Player* by Caravaggio, 1596. (Hermitage version). https://commons.wikimedia.org/wiki/File:Caravaggio,_Michelangelo_Merisi_d a_-_The_Lute-Player.jpg

Back cover image: Portrait d'Émile Nelligan in 1899. Laprés & Lavergne. *Archives de la Ville de Montréal* BM1-5P1570-03. https://ville.montreal.qc.ca/ memoiresdesmontrealais/emile-nelligan-ou-labime-du-reve

Softcover 978-1-989048-77-1
Digital 978-1-989048-76-4

A5: 5-7/8" x 8-1/4" / 148 x 210 mm
Times New Roman 10/12
Gill Sans 10, 16
ca. 39,000 words
8 illustrations
50 lb paper, creme
186 pages
R1

Editing and design
Peter Geldart, Danielle Michaud Aubrey
Petra Books 2023
petrabooks.ca

# Contents

# Selected Verse of Émile Nelligan

# Introduction

*Poetic fever*

Émile Nelligan was a brilliant and neurotic late-adolescent poet of Irish-*Canadien* background writing in French in late 19th-century Montréal. He lived from 1879 to 1941. Perhaps the best quick description of his poetry is melancholy lyricism. He published his first poems in 1896 at age 16. By the summer of 1899 he had published a couple dozen poems, with 150 more in varied condition in his notebooks. At this point, at the peak of his poetic fever, he suffered a mental breakdown. He spent the remaining forty-two years of his life in asylums, producing no new poems, but remembering the old ones.

As Nelligan's poetry and personal story became widely known during the early 20th century, especially since the 1930s, his fame grew until he achieved mythic status in French Canada, where he represented Lost Youth, Mad Genius, the Crucified One. Schools are named for him. Monuments stand in his memory. No other poet in Canada has been the subject of so many biographies, films, novels, plays, and critical debates. Several of his poems have been put to music.

Nelligan has been called Canada's first modern poet, counting both English and French Canada. He was modern in the sense of poeticizing his personal neurotic issues. Today's readers, however, might be surprised to find him expressing these issues in sonnets and rondels.

Readers in English unfamiliar with Nelligan's story will surely find this meteoric figure, this psychological case lodged within Quebec culture, an illuminating discovery. The poems selected for this book will help articulate that story, at the same time as they demonstrate that Nelligan was a musician of words who deserves to be better known beyond Québec's borders.

*Terroir*

Émile was born in Montréal on Christmas Eve, 1879, first fruit of the marriage between Émilie Hudon and David Nelligan four years earlier. During the years that mattered most for Émile's poetry, the family (including his younger sisters, Éva and Gertrude) lived at the northern edge of the city in what was then a middle-class area, on avenue Laval a short stroll from carré St.-Louis, the park where today stands a bronze bust of Nelligan.

His life unfolds in a French Canadian hyper-Catholic culture mostly lost now. Schools and hospitals are run by religious orders. Pupils learn the catechism. Impure thoughts are a sin. If you die with a mortal sin on your soul, you go to Hell. The liturgical calendar is vigorous — Lent, Good Friday, the feast days of the saints, and so on. The public fills the pews at Mass; they line up at the confessionals. It was another world.

It was in this fashion that, since the English Conquest of New France in 1760, an arch-conservative clergy had soldiered on, the imagery of Heaven and Hell at their disposal, keeping the French flock in a religious uniform distinct from the infidel conquerors.

As to a specific case like Nelligan, it's easy to see that the religion of his time and place did him more harm than good. It seems to have evoked in him a world of angels and demons. And you need not search far in his poetry to find the Holy Mother/Blessed Virgin dichotomy shaping his women. One reason for Quebec's prolonged interest in Nelligan, I suspect, is that he is a sort of horror museum of the Quebec Catholic psychoscape.

Nelligan was a symbolist poet, which might throw light on why Catholic mythology is so personal and overwhelming for him: the Holy Mother is the motherliness of his own mother. Baby Jesus equals swaddling infantine Bliss. Jesus on the cross is Émile the Sufferer.

But Émile drew upon pre-Christian deities as well — because they too were symbols that told his story. Pan, the randy flute-playing wildman. Icarus, symbol of flying too high on man-made wings. And most of all Venus-Aphrodite who, as we shall see, calls the poet to sensual love, luring him to his doom.

### Poète maudit

Émile's juvenile years were particularly difficult. He attended a series of French Catholic schools and was a poor student, a fact usually attributed to daydreaming and long absences. At age 15, one unexplained absence stretched six months, from September 1895 when he failed to appear for the start of the school year, up to March 1896 when he finally made it to class.

Still, it was in this environment that poetry infected him. The first poets he encountered were the routine French Romantics that were acceptable for school books. Away from school he uncovered other sources. The Montreal journals, of which there was a plethora, occasionally printed work by French avant-garde poets such as Charles Baudelaire or Paul Verlaine. Nelligan read a furtive copy of Baudelaire's *Les Fleurs du mal* during a family vacation at

Cacouna, a beach town on the lower St. Lawrence. That was 1896. He was age 16. Around this time or a bit before, he discovered Arthur Rimbaud and other Parisian *poètes maudits* as well.

Paris, by the way, is part of this story. Paris was Nelligan's beacon. Paris was where poets were lionized, where a book of verse could be a best-seller.

It was in that same year 1896 that the first trickle of Émile's own poetry appeared in the weekly journal *Le Samedi* above the pen name Émile Kovar, that last name possibly inspired by the popular stage play *Paul Kauvar*. The Kauvar character is a valiant French revolutionary leader who, bidding farewell to his sweet wife, is marched to the guillotine but is saved at the last moment when news arrives that the Great Terror has ended.

After failing his mid-term exams, Nelligan dropped out of school in February 1897, intending to become a poet. He immediately joined a literary club, the École Littéraire de Montréal, that gave him opportunities to discuss and recite poetry with other poets. This club became legendary mainly because Nelligan had joined it; read more about that in the remarks on "Wine Song" (poem 37).

Thus began what is called Nelligan's bohemian phase, which entailed hanging out with fellow poets in cafés, sharing absinthe in garrets, wandering the city and composing verse, without much in visible means of support. Given that Émile was still living at home with his parents, however, bohemianism was bound to cause friction.

### Nelligan's women

Many of Émile's poems are expressly or otherwise about women; here I'll touch on the key female characters in his poetry.

To start with, there's the Shepherdess, bucolic companion of Nelligan's early pastoral phase. She dies, cause unknown. Is she a real person or merely a symbol of pastoralism? We'll look into the riddle of the Shepherdess in the Comments to the poem titled "Shepherdess" (poem 5).

Next comes Gretchen, the *famous* Gretchen, as they say in Québec Lit, where she is a renowned mystery. Émile is head-over-heels about her in "Placet" (poem 16). But when the fling ends, in "Gretchen the Pale" (poem 21) she is a Venus made of cold marble.

The third romantic interest is a known person, a historical certainty: Robertine Barry, often referred to as "Françoise", her pen name in the journal *La Patrie* where as a culture maven she published some of Nelligan's poems. Robertine hosted salons at her lodgings on rue Saint-Denis where Émile would drop in, air his latest verses, and borrow the literary reviews she received from Paris. He thought that in Robertine he had found a soulmate. One day, inevitably, he proposed something — marriage, one assumes, though some writers instead picture Émile making an impetuous physical advance. She turned him down. After that he wrote bitter poems about her, just as he had about Gretchen.

It's time now to mention the important consideration that Robertine was sixteen years older than Nelligan. In addition, she was a friend of his mother's. Virtually every commentary on Nelligan places oedipal issues at the heart of the poet's psychological disarray.

His mother was Émilie Amanda Hudon, a Kamouraska girl with a gift for the piano. Émile took his musicality from her. She is said to have been devout and church-going. In 1875, at age 19 she married David Nelligan, age 26, a postal inspector for the fledgling Dominion of Canada government. David had arrived in Montreal at age 8 when his parents emigrated from Ireland.

While his mother appears in many of Émile's poems, his father David appears in just one, "The Traveler", composed probably in early 1897, and printed in the journal *Le Monde illustré* in October of that year. The poem, not included in this selection, has a dutiful air. Émile specifically dedicated it to his father, whose job as an inspector made him a traveler. The poem ends with the winter winds whisking the traveler into the night on a final voyage. Émile may have been aiming for a vaguely affectionate and mystical effect, but my guess is that at home the poem went over like a lead balloon. Would *père* not suspect that those whisking winds were meant to say, "Begone with you"?

## The De Marchy Crisis

On the face of it, the year 1899 does not begin badly for Nelligan, age 19. He has a (to him) plausible career path. His poetry has appeared in several journals. He has recited with the literary club in public forums. Above all, an idea is growing in his mind: he will publish a book — in Paris! He initially plans to call it *Songs of the Angels*.

In March, he sits for a professional photograph at the shop of Laprés & Lavergne on rue Saint-Denis. The picture is well-known. Émile with his superb head of hair looks at once Byronic and moonstruck — practically a parody of a Romantic poet. But he's well-dressed, wearing a starchy white collar, a firm overcoat, he looks believable as a rising literary personality.

The histories (see Bibliography) generally point now to what I will call the De Marchy Crisis, precipitated by a review of one of the literary club's public recitals that appeared in *Le Monde illustré* in that same month of March. The reviewer, Édouard de Marchy, a visiting journalist from Paris, gives Nelligan a dismissive paragraph at the foot of his article. Nelligan's problem, de Marchy says, is lack of originality, and he clumsily associates Émile with the image of a multi-colored parrot, implying that the poet mimics an assortment of other poets — Parisian poets, presumably.

Nelligan was devastated. De Marchy may have touched a nerve (we'll get to that later). What must have stung worst of all was that de Marchy was from Paris, the capital of poetry. The balloon had burst. After two years of living the dream of being a *poète maudit*, Émile suffers a crisis of confidence. From here on, his poems will be about failure and shattered hopes. We'll say more about the De Marchy Crisis in the Comments to "Wine Song" (poem 37).

### Summer 1899 breakdown

David Nelligan, Émile's father, likely was at the end of his patience. Émile seemed incapable of holding a job, incapable even of wanting a job. There is a tradition, based on the recollections of one of Émile's cousins, that David in 1898 obtained a position for his son aboard a ship to Liverpool and back, but biographer Paul Wyczynski, scouring the port archives in both Montréal and Liverpool, found no supporting evidence. It could be that the young man simply did not show up for departure. That same year David purportedly wangled a clerical post for his son, only to see Émile quit after a ridiculously short time. It may be that Émile is so powerfully driven to write poetry that it is not possible to humbly concentrate on other tasks; one's artistic nature is bursting to be fulfilled.

Then came the Robertine fiasco. His parents must have heard about it, she being a friend of his mother. The episode occurred probably in late spring of 1899, when Émile was in a forlorn mood and Robertine was caringly printing him in *La Patrie* to keep his spirits up. Robertine's rebuff to Émile's romantic overture is often taken as one of the last straws contributing to his breakdown.

Living at home was viable for Émile only because his father was often away on the postal inspection circuit. When David returned, Émile made himself scarce, taking shelter with a relative or friend, or else, some say, wandering the streets, sleeping on benches, lining up for soup handouts.

His father, unsupportive of his son's career as a dreamer, inevitably becomes the go-to villain of the story. André Vanasse in a fictionalized biography, *Nelligan: le spasme de vivre*, portrays David Nelligan as an alcoholic and a sporadic wife-beater. More often the man is presented as a stock bourgeois *paterfamilias*, a *maudit Anglais* in all but name. English was spoken as a rule when he was at home. Yet he spoke French well enough to maintain his inspection territory in largely francophone Gaspésie, and he accepted that his son be raised in French schools — despite Émile's poor record.

The father is said to have blamed the mother for mollycoddling the boy. Certainly Madame Nelligan was more open to the notion that Émile had some art to accomplish. Her son had been poetic since age 13 when he performed at church socials. But surely by summer of 1899 Madame Nelligan was growing alarmed. It's reasonable to ask why her hard-line husband didn't once and for all kick his *bon à rien* son out of the house. The answer is probably that Émile clearly had a nervous condition. In fact he had a history. We know that Émile had visited a psychiatric clinic in 1898, but we lack details. In one of his poems, *Les angéliques*, he admitted to owning "a flock of neuroses".

Louis Dantin, the fallen priest who became Nelligan's first editor, concluded that Neurosis was the engine of Nelligan's poetic mission. Dantin capitalized "Neurosis", as if to make it a deity. But it's not as if Nelligan was profiting from this drive in him, it's not as if he was sailing happily through life. His disorder was clearly in this summer of 1899 carrying him to self-destruction.

In June or July his father enrolled Émile in a reform school operated by the Frères de la Charité that was oriented toward behavioral issues. Not much is known about that period. At home, Nelligan would shut himself in his room, writing feverishly, in principle going full-out on the book, but more and more documenting his breakdown as it happened. The poetry of this phase is filled with literary as well as psychological interest exemplified by such dark mileposts as "The Crows" (poem 43) and "Nocturnal Confession" (poem 44).

He was under the influence of the "Decadent" poets now, the likes of Georges Rodenbach and Maurice Rollinat, who had a penchant for horror features such as skeletons playing the piano; they were the sort of abandoned souls who figured that in this unkind world one might as well do morphine.

It was a catastrophic summer for Émile. According to Dantin, the young poet sequestered himself in his room for entire days, his thoughts delirious.

He suffered hallucinations and nightmares whose impact might have been all the more powerful insofar as symbols were the language of his dreams. At night, angel-girls, lover-girls, succubae came to visit him. From the evidence of "The Crows", he may have experienced physical spasms.

Was there some specific incident where the poet's mind finally cracked? He had certainly contemplated suicide in his verse — did he bring himself to the point of actually doing it? Or was it a matter of his becoming ever more withdrawn and non-functional from day to day? On August 9, an otherwise pleasant summer day at 25°C according to weather records, Nelligan was transported by carriage east along rue Notre-Dame to rural Longue-Pointe where he was deposited at la Retraite St.-Benoît, a mental asylum. Émile's father had signed the committal papers a few days before.

*Diagnosis*

The diagnosis by the doctors who admitted Nelligan to St.-Benoît was "*dégénérescence mentale et folie polymorphe*," terms that signified schizophrenia and hallucinations while pointing to genetic and neurological causes. However, it is interesting to look at some aspects of the case.

Dantin in his preface to *Émile Nelligan et son Œuvre* offered analogies for the poet's breakdown. "Perhaps the lyre must snap after attempting," said Dantin, "the symphonies of the beyond". This mystical angle contrasted with the more psychological reading he had offered just a few lines earlier where he said "The butterfly burns in the flame of its dream". Some biographers suggest that Émile chose his destiny. He identified with a Romantic caricature, the poetic soul doomed to madness or suicide in a cruel world. They say he took to heart Rimbaud's advice to derange one's senses to reach the Unknown.

Today we're inclined to look for underlying conditions. If one chooses to go mad, that choice would itself be a symptom of madness. The willingness to follow an inner demon might be inspired by Rimbaud, but it might at the same time be an aspect of one's illness.

How long had the disease been percolating in him? From conception, from the cosmos, some readers might contend. From childhood, at least. It was there in the daydreaming, in the truancies. In the visions of golden boyhood. He had a blockage: he did not want to enter adulthood, a state clearly inferior to youth.

I find it hard to avoid the reflection that, whatever its organic and psychiatric basis, madness was for Nelligan an exit from his problems, an economic solution, a means to survive in some faint form after his whole life had become untenable. He did become the exalted name he had wanted to be; but by the same token he was no longer fundamentally engaged in the quest for fame.

As we shall learn, there are varying conjectures as to what specifically led to Nelligan's internment and what procedures he was subjected to when there.

*Asylum years*

La Retraite St.-Benoît was a private 150-room hospital run by les Frères de la Charité, the Brothers of Charity. The Brothers ran the reform school where David had enrolled Émile not long before, and also operated this rural haven for intractable cases. David Nelligan paid $20 per month to maintain his son there, not including extra charges for toiletries and clothing. It would be a notable expense for Mr. Nelligan, who after 1906 lived on an annual pension of $1,240.

The accommodation at St.-Benoît was comfortable. Nelligan had a room to himself, there was an armchair to read in, a table to write at. The institution had a large garden overlooking the St. Lawrence, where it is said that Émile liked to watch ships passing to and from the sea.

His case might have been manageable by today's science, with pills for instance. But back in his day, there wasn't much room for hope. Poor Nelligan, his colleagues said, *pauvre Nelligan!* Dantin, who in 1900 visited Nelligan in the asylum for the one and only time, concluded that Émile's condition was terminal. His eyes may be open, his heart may beat, Dantin announced, but Émile Nelligan is dead.

Madame Nelligan likewise visited just once, which is harder to explain. She became a depressed personality in later life; but then of course she had Émile to be depressed about. She died in 1913. Émile's dad, who lived to 1924, never visited at all.

But we do hear word of Émile from time to time during his long internment. There are reports of him in agony, others of him lost in dream.

Ernest Choquette, a medical doctor, visited the poet in 1909 and reported to the journal *Le Canada* that he found Nelligan practically unrecognizable, slumped lifelessly on a bench, until finally after some coaxing the poet sprang to life and recited perfectly from memory a long poem before a room full of dead-eyed patients, some of them crying or shouting in corners.

Albert Lozeau, a literary club member who had also visited the asylum, seemed to believe that Nelligan had undergone a lobotomy. "That a steel sacrilege would dig into your brain..." begins his outraged sonnet "To Émile Nelligan" published in the journal *Le Nationaliste* in January 1910.

There is a photo of Émile circa 1920, which would be his twenty-first year in St.-Benoît asylum. His back is against a stone wall, apparently outdoors. His folded arms, tensed shoulders and tightly-wrapped scarf keep him determinedly closed off from us; there's grief and alarm and defiance on his face. The camera is a threat to him.

After his father's death in 1925, with no one willing to pay Nelligan's continued keep at St.-Benoît, he was sent to l'Hôpital Saint-Jean-de-Dieu, where he remained a ward of the government until his death. Saint-Jean had 3,000 patients. Nelligan shared a dorm with thirty of them. In this phase he seems to have been docile. He was trusted to push the linen cart. Journalists and students visited him. There is a story that he conducted a poetry soirée with violin accompaniment for his fellow inmates. He could still recite the old poetry, but in a monotone voice, so visitors said. Dressed in jacket and tie, he understood that he counted for something in the outside world, but he accepted that he belonged in the asylum, being maintained as a sort of living monument to poetry.

If any new poems emerged from Nelligan during all these years, they have vanished. Instead, he copied and recopied from memory his own past poems and those of other poets. Sometimes, it is illuminating to note, he invented variations on the old poems with clever portmanteau words, such as *horbeaux* (horribows) for *horribles corbeaux* (horrible crows).

Living in these institutions was nevertheless life under the Catholic umbrella. A doctor at L'Hôpital St.-Jean-de-Dieu told Paul Wyczynski that Émile had a practice of visiting the hospital chapel to gaze upon and speak to the statue of the Blessed Virgin.

We might wish that Nelligan had recovered, that he had rebounded to the 'real' world to provide more poetry. But would his poetic drive have rebounded with him? Some people are creative only in the conditions of some particular phase of their life.

Émile's physical health declined noticeably starting in 1939. There were multiple problems: lungs, prostate, heart. The doctors fed him digitalis to keep that weary heart beating. On 18 November 1941, at age 61, Émile Nelligan left this world. A death mask was made, and he was buried in Cimetière Notre-Dame-des-Neiges.

# Controversies

A number of controversies have raged in Quebec literary circles with regard to Nelligan's character and worthiness.

*Was Nelligan original?*

De Marchy's devastating criticism in *Le Monde illustré* was that Nelligan was more parrot than poet. The ascension of Nelligan to the status of *poète national* in the 20th century may have made de Marchy look like a false prophet, but nevertheless some critics have continued, like de Marchy, to see Nelligan as an imitator.

There's no denying the enormous influence Parisian poets had on him. Nelligan memorized them, absorbed them, emulated them. At that age, of course he would emulate. When he was writing, inevitably their images, sometimes even their rhyme schemes, welled up in his mind. You might say he was doing variations on the masters. How far should we push the question, though? Practically every image might come from someone else. That rain, from Baudelaire; that bell, from Rodenbach.

In his asylum years, Nelligan was known to sign his name to other poets' poems, and to sign their names to his own. Poetry was all one big ball of wax.

It will be helpful to review what sort of poet Nelligan is. He combines a number of currents, but he is fundamentally a symbolist, which is to say that he advances a constellation of symbolic meanings. For example, a garden is Eden. A country chapel is simple faith. If the chapel is in ruins, well, you can guess what that means.

Symbols are like a natural resource, generally available to all users. Nelligan felt free to pluck symbols from the symbolist treasure-chest and deploy them to his own ends in his own verses.

Nelligan personally considered himself not so much a Symbolist as a Parnassian, a category that had more *cachet*. The Parnassians were the cool school of 19th-century poetry, the zealots of tight form and compressed meanings. The motto *l'art pour l'art* often associated with the movement is usually translated as "art for art's sake," which doesn't quite capture the fanatical idealism entailed. The Parnassians took their name from sacred Mount Parnassus, home of the Delphic oracle.

Generally, the distinctive mix you get in Nelligan is this: Nelligan the Symbolist displays his symbols while Nelligan the Parnassian sculpts them.

At the end, in that fateful summer of 1899, Nelligan the Decadent drives his symbols into brilliant psychotic depths.

Nelligan combined the borrowed aspects of his poetry with original and personal aspects, and he did that with superb musicality. Dantin, responsible for introducing the poet to the wider public with his 1904 compilation *Émile Nelligan et son Œuvre,* described Nelligan as "a great musician of syllables".

Nelligan's work in his final creative days, approaching the breakdown, is dramatic and obsessive to an extent you are not likely to have witnessed in poetry before. Assuredly, Nelligan deserves to be recognized for the unique configuration that he is.

## Was he gay?

It would not be surprising if in his so-called bohemian days certain inferences were made regarding Nelligan's sexuality. For one thing, his Parisian idols, Verlaine and Rimbaud, were models of debauchery. Nelligan has been labelled "the Canadian Rimbaud," a sobriquet that satisfies the idea of a brilliant meteoric career, but also hints at sexual deviance.

Once Nelligan was cloistered in an asylum and then elevated to the rank of national poet, his sins, whatever they were, were as good as forgotten. But in the sexually liberated air of the late 20th century, a number of mostly fiction writers, sensing that the time had come to de-sanitize Nelligan's reputation, latched onto the idea that some of Émile's comrades were, or might have been, bisexual or homosexual. In particular they pointed to Arthur de Bussières, a fellow poet remembered nowadays only for being a character in Nelligan's story. He was two years older than Émile and had the same first name as Rimbaud.

The typical seduction scenario has Émile fleeing an oppressive home environment to take refuge in Arthur's garret. Michel Tremblay, in his libretto for the opera *Nelligan* performed in Montréal in 1990, has Émile succumbing to a steamy de Bussières then crying out to the world for acceptance, while Émile's family and friends wail that the poet has gone mad. In *Portrait de Nelligan Déchiré,* a 1992 "dramatic fiction" by Aude Nantais and Jean-Joseph Tremblay, the future national poet ends up peddling himself to sailors in port taverns.

Author Bernard Courteau beginning with his 1986 *Nelligan n'était pas fou!* ("Nelligan Wasn't Crazy!") launched a series of literary speculations that concluded that homosexuality was a factor, perhaps the main factor, behind the decision to intern the poet. A curious thing about St.-Benoît, the asylum where Nelligan's father sent him, was that it was partly a place where the Church consigned priests afflicted with alcoholism and/or what was labelled *déviance sexuelle* — sexual deviation.

The proposition that homosexuality played a role in Nelligan's life could answer some irksome questions, such as why exactly do people disdain the poet in "Wine Song" (poem 37) and other poems? Homosexuality might be the stigma that explains why his parents stayed away after Émile was relegated to St.-Benoît.

For all that, let's remind ourselves that the gay thesis consists of no more than speculation and fiction-writing, real-life evidence being unavailable. It's the sort of proposition that can only rile a veteran biographer such as Paul Wyczynski (*Nell. Bio.*) who protests that in thirty-five years of research on Nelligan he discovered no trace of sexual deviation. "Let those who say otherwise provide proofs!"

Nelligan, of course, need not be gay for having comrades who were. For a repressed personality in a repressed society, the openness to sexual options, even the awareness of them, might be surprisingly limited.

A major challenge for the gay thesis is the obvious heterosexual orientation of Nelligan's verses. To the last he places Venus on the prow of his soaring, symbolic ship of gold (see poem 45).

Taking the material at face value, Émile's poetry consistently points to frustrated *heterosexual* desire. What we find is a young man who feels the expected juvenile mating pressure, shaped though it is by particular psychological factors. It is this poetic drama that is, by and large, the subject of this book.

Was there something more? Was there some detour or some incident? That line of thought has been left to the realm of novels and plays.

### Was he anti-Semitic?

Although I've not seen this particular controversy raised elsewhere, I would be remiss not to mention that Nelligan uses the word *juif* (Jew) in two poems, and in each case an accusation of anti-Semitism might be brought. I've left those poems out of this book because, frankly, they are not particularly spirited or engaging verses; but here in summary is what they say:

Nelligan's poem *L'Antiquaire* ("The Pawnbroker"), composed probably in 1898 or earlier, presents an avaricious shopkeeper — a modern Shylock, the poet calls him — who roams his glittering shop like a lost soul, rolling an ample jewel between his fingers, till suddenly he recoils in horror at the discovery that his prized Louis XIV ring is no more than a bauble. Someone has deceived him, then. The allusion to Louis XIV, presumably based on that king's admission of Jews into France centuries ago, feels too erudite to spring from Nelligan unaided. Be that as it may, the poem's emphasis is not on cupidity so much as on the *forsakenness* of the merchant, an approach that takes for granted a negative myth of the Wandering Jew forever condemned for making a Wrong Choice.

The second poem is titled *Les Déicides* ("The God Killers") and it appeared in Louis Dantin's pious *Petit Messager* magazine in October 1898. It's actually a double sonnet, the kind of offering Dantin utilized to fill the two-page spreads he liked to run. In the first sonnet, Nelligan has the Jews mocking Jesus, whereupon God tears apart their temple curtain, and ever since then the Jews wander Christendom like the ghosts of the damned, finding ghettos instead of homeland, receiving insults instead of kindness.

But might this not be a criticism of Christians, for whom Charity is deemed a primary virtue? In the second sonnet, accordingly, Nelligan shifts the definition of "God-killers" to include Christians who torture Christ with their sins and faithlessness. One day, he says, these infidels will plunge into eternal damnation, a satanic mark on their brow designating *them* as the God-killers.

Context is important. Anti-Semitism was on the rise in late 19th-century Western societies. In Quebec it garnered support among some clergy and in the press. Though officially the Catholic Church had long ago rejected the position that the Jewish people were "God-killers" responsible for Christ's crucifixion, the accusation continued to thrive in extreme Catholic journals such as the laughably-named *La Vérité* ("The Truth") in Quebec City. Some mainstream publications were willing to maintain the drumbeat. *Le Monde illustré* evidently considered it acceptable discourse in February 1899 when their literary critic from Paris, Édouard de Marchy, in a rant against the trend to *décadence* in literature, squarely put the blame on Jewish financiers who, led by "the Rothschilds and their accomplices", were plotting in their synagogues the ruination of France and the Catholic faith.

Like everyone, Nelligan was a creature of society. Whatever else he wished to say in "The Pawnbroker", the use of the term "modern Shylock" is today a glaring racial slur. The term may have come reflexively to the poet in that time and place. As for "The God Killers", in this case we know that the poem was the brainchild of the poet's friend and mentor Dantin, who said as much himself in later years. He had challenged Nelligan to a contest to see which of the two could create the best poem on the subject. Nelligan won.

But why was Dantin interested in this particular theme? One of the founding aims of the Fathers of the Blessed Sacrament was to move Catholicism more toward a religion of love. Therefore the strongly-rooted notion of Christ sentencing a whole people to abuse for all eternity was intellectually awkward; the topic deserved to be explored.

For its time and place, "The God Killers" might have been one of those soft steps in a liberal direction that ordinary people can make in a rigid environment, in this case offering the magazine's pious readers a new angle, new equivalences to consider, in their attitude toward Jews.

And as we shall see, the issue of being a faithless Christian was on Dantin's mind since, wretch that he was, he was living in Holy Orders though his faith had crumbled.

### What was Louis Dantin's role?

A dispute that flares regularly in Quebec literary circles concerns how much, if any, of the Nelligan oeuvre ought to be attributed to Louis Dantin, whose collection *Émile Nelligan et son Œuvre* made the young poet in the asylum famous.

Dantin is an intricate subject in his own right. His real name was Eugène Seers, raised in Beauharnois, west of Montreal. Fourteen years older than Nelligan, Seers had studied in Paris and Rome, and took his vows as a priest with the Fathers of the Blessed Sacrament in Brussels. The Fathers were a Eucharistic cult whose premise was that God's love, channeled through the communion wafer (the Host), will make a Christ of each of us, thereby achieving Christ's Kingdom on Earth. But at age 28 Seers came under a cloud when he developed an "attachment" (his word) to a 16-year-old Belgian girl. Simultaneously, he lost his religious faith. The situation was delicate since Seers came from a family of lavish donors. The Fathers found a spot for him back in Canada.

Louis Dantin was the *nom de plume* by which Eugène Seers eventually became known. Students of Quebec literature will want to recognize both of his names, but for simplicity I'll stick with Dantin.

Dantin befriended Nelligan probably in summer 1898 at which time Dantin was dwelling in the priests' residence on avenue Mont-Royal, where in an adjunct to the residence he operated the priestly print shop. Dantin had an eye open for promising poets since he was charged with publishing the congregation's pious magazine, *Le Petit Messager du Très Saint Sacrement,* the Little Messenger of the Blessed Sacrament.

Nelligan and Dantin met often to discuss poetry, in the lounge of the sacredotal residence but also at poetry readings and on walks. There can be little doubt that Dantin inspired or even cooked up ideas for a number of Nelligan's pious poems, and this involvement has been enough to foster an image of Dantin as *puppetmeister*.

At this point we should mention that 1) a magazine editor might well develop ideas in person with prospective contributors, and 2) Nelligan's ability to possess a pious frame of mind fluctuated over time and did not endure. The poet would soon suffer the agonized loss of faith exhibited in "The Bell in the Fog" (poem 25) and "Christ on the Cross" (poem 26).

After Nelligan's internment, Dantin pleaded with Nelligan's mother to permit him to gather the poet's manuscripts into a book, into *the* book that Émile had always wanted. Dantin labored on the project for two years, clandestinely, in the Fathers' print shop, eventually assembling *Émile Nelligan et son Œuvre* before returning the poet's papers to Madame Nelligan. The latter may not have cared to preserve the papers, because much of the original material vanished, which in turn created room for critics to allege that Nelligan's verses had benefited from *rewrites* by Dantin.

At the extreme are those who make Dantin the true creator of Nelligan's poetry. For, the argument goes, how can it be that Nelligan the high-school dropout produces such exquisite verses, replete with Latin phrases and Greek cities? Dantin, being a savant, was therefore the likely author.

The squabble is Québec's equivalent to the mystery of who really wrote Shakespeare. The inquiry was revived most recently by Yvette Francoli in *Le Naufragé du Vaisseau d'or* ("The Castaway of the Ship of Gold"), a biography intent on exposing the "secret lives" of Louis Dantin.

But it is not enough to contend, as Francoli does, that Dantin, a master of pseudonyms, is precisely the sort of trickster who would enjoy using Nelligan's name as cover for his own versifying. There needs to be real textual proof showing Dantin red-handedly forging or usurping a Nelligan poem. And there isn't. The worst that is known about Dantin's editorial work is that he moderated some of Nelligan's words that potentially would offend the Church and embarrass Madame Nelligan. In that regard, see the Comments for "Monks in File" (poem 9) and "Ecclesiastical Siesta" (poem 20).

Moreover, it's wrong to think of Nelligan's education as if it had been a waste of time. His marks in languages had been good. And he gained knowledge from all the poetry he read. One could learn a lot about mythology from French poets.

There were witnesses, including Robertine Barry, who had read or heard Émile's poetry freshly created. Some poems penned in Nelligan's hand survive. In that category I include those poems he wrote from memory in the asylum; the fact that he could reproduce them into his old age suggests that the compositions were enshrined in his mind more firmly than if they had been the creations of someone else.

Dantin maintained to the day he died that his contribution to Nelligan's poetry was minimal, even as a mentor. As he remembered it, Nelligan never much followed his advice. As an editor, Dantin said he simply did the sorting, correcting, and occasional discrete polishing that the job normally requires.

Dantin was himself a writer of verse, but he felt that his own skills fell short of Nelligan's. He was right about that. Dantin's verse, stiff and intellectual, conspicuously lacks Nelligan's music and youthful fire.

There is no denying that Dantin in another respect was essential to Nelligan's success. It was Dantin who shaped the legend of Nelligan, the legend of the Québec prodigy from whose tongue verse flowed as if poured from an invisible realm. That effort succeeded so well that Nelligan was touted as Québec's "*poète national*" well into the 20th century. To be sure, the title is honorific, awarded by general literary assent to various gifted poets over the years, but it positions Nelligan in the loftiest circle of the Québec cultural firmament.

# Notes on Translation

I had not heard of Émile Nelligan until I encountered Jean-Paul Lemieux's astute painting *Hommage à Nelligan* some years ago. It's a large picture, 133 cm wide. The subject is a young man, bowler-hatted, bundled in an overcoat, standing stiff as a penguin before a wintry twilight park. At first glance he resembles some overwrought accountant. How was this tremulous figure with the Irish family name worthy of the homage of this prominent Québec artist?

Eventually from casual investigation I learned that Nelligan was a significant poet and Québec cultural icon. I found his lyrical poetry clever and refreshing, and his life story psychologically intriguing. I translated four of his poems for an article in the *Spadina Literary Review* some time ago, and, evidently enjoying the task, I translated several more poems in subsequent years. What struck me most about Nelligan was his dexterity with such rule-based forms as the sonnet and the rondel. I felt that his poetry had a level of elegance and musicality that is not often matched by poetry today and deserves, at the minimum, to be remembered.

## Fixed forms

Nelligan has been called Canada's first modern poet, which is true enough in the sense that putting your neuroses on display is modern. But at the same time this poet adheres to traditional, ultimately medieval, lyrical forms.

Nearly half of his poems are sonnets. Fourteen lines long, the sonnet traces back at least to the Age of Chivalry, when it was literally a "little song" about one's idealized ladylove. The sonnet gained wider application in subsequent centuries, until eventually no topic was beyond its reach. Nelligan favored the "alexandrine sonnet" wherein each line consists of twelve syllables divided by a mid-line *caesura*. The term *caesura* is customarily translated as "pause," which is not wrong but sometimes it is helpful to think of it as a beat, a tonal or rhythmic crest halfway through the line.

The rondel was more demanding still — thirteen lines built on just two rhymes, with certain lines repeated — but it produced irresistible resonances and closed-loop effects. Accomplishing a rondel is a *tour de force*.

Here, then, was formal rigor of a kind you don't see any more. And it was coming from a kid who was a nervous wreck.

*Lyricism*

The forty-six Nelligan poems in this collection come from an extant oeuvre of approximately 170 poems. Generally I selected poems on the basis of their lyrical and psychological interest, and, not least of all, their ability to tell Nelligan's story. I have been sure to include touchstone poems such as "Wine Song" (poem 37) and "The Ship of Gold" (poem 45). Every poem comes with Notes and/or Comments, some brief, others more elaborate. Following the translations is an appendix with Nelligan's poems in French. The poems are numbered for easy cross-reference between English and French versions.

Only about a quarter of Nelligan's poems have documented dates for being recited or published prior to his entry into an asylum. The rest were found on papers he left behind. Louis Dantin's compilation of 1904 organized the poems by literary and intellectual categories rather than chronologically. I was grateful to read the 1991 book *Nelligan amoureux* by Pierre Lemieux who developed a chronological framework by aligning Nelligan's poems with amorous experiences that were deduced from the words themselves.

I have also learned much from other biographers and critics such as Paul Wyczynski, Emile Talbot, and Réjean Robidoux.

The ordering and numbering of poems in this book do not correspond to any plan of Nelligan's. I have arranged the poems in what seems to me a credible semi-chronological order, placing them along a trajectory based on what is known or guessable about the poet's life and influences. Sometimes, however, I shuffled the order to bring out affinities, or alternatively, to demonstrate variety.

Nelligan's most nerve-wracked work, the poetry of his imminent breakdown, naturally comes at the end of the selection.

For the most part when I talk about Nelligan in this book, I have in mind the creative Nelligan, the pre-breakdown Nelligan. The gangly lad bent over his writing table or gesticulating with ink-stained hands at the poetry readings. I go along with most of his biographers in interpreting Nelligan's poetry as if he is telling the story of himself. His breakdown, as it were, certified the story told in his verses.

I have tried to stay faithful to Nelligan's meters and rhyme schemes while keeping the meanings clear. A simple lyricism was what I hoped to convey in these translations. Even in his greatest distress, Nelligan is not Nelligan without his perfect sonnets and rondels.

~~~

Selected Verse of Émile Nelligan

# 46 Poems Translated into English
# with Commentary

# 1. Like a Shepherd

Like holy orisons sweet breezes did play
And the sound of the flute faded softly away.

The cattle are home, they moo in the stable
While on steamy hot soup we feast at the table.

Now off to bed, boyo. O Pan, say your prayers!
Let your hard-working arms set aside their affairs.

The moonlight wafts down on the silken terrain.
O sleep! Come give me your joyous kiss again.

In the night a dog barks, as to slumber I part,
Sweet dreams come to knock at the door of my heart.

How delicious it was in those days to be free,
To live life like a shepherd. Yes, within me

That memory tingles still. Back when I was a boy,
Far from the beaten paths, life was pure and full of joy.

### Notes

LINE 5: *Pan.* Ancient Greek god of flocks, fields and forests — a nature spirit. But here the term is meant as an affectionate sobriquet for the herd boy.

### *Comments*

A rare product from Nelligan — a happy poem. Or at least a memory of happy times. This is Nelligan in his pastoral phase.

Pastoral poetry is probably as old as civilization. It certainly thrived in Europe since the Renaissance, presenting a mostly urban audience with an idealized countryside where shepherds and shepherdesses, their sheep-minding chores not overly onerous, cavort to the sound of flutes.

"Like a Shepherd" is a pastoral poem in the "Virgilian" mode, that is, evoking a tone of nostalgic regret for the simple rural life such as the poet Virgil (70-19 BCE) expressed in his 2,000-line *Georgics*.

This is a major theme in Nelligan, that a personal golden age of childhood bliss has been inconsolably lost. When I was a boy, he says, life was full of joy.

~ ~ ~

## 2. Watteau Dream

Back when the goatherds, in crimson eventide,
Guiding their big black bucks as golden panpipes played,
Past acres where hollies stood in rows arrayed,
Over hills and back to their native hamlet plied:

Vagabond school kids, souls that never a battle made,
Full of blank yesterday, no rancor borne inside,
Skipping school, through woods where nutshells lay strewn wide
We ambled, goofing round, harkening to the cascade

Of falling brooks in the valley where yapping ran
The little sheepdog of these placid sons of Pan
Whose melancholy pipe calls from far away.

Then, exhausted, shivering from cold, we went to bed,
And sometimes, glorying in our palaces of hay,
We breakfasted on dawn and supped on stars overhead.

_Notes_

TITLE: Antoine Watteau (1684-1721) was a French painter of bucolic scenes. A "Watteau dream" here would be a country idyll. Nelligan knew something about painting thanks to his acquaintance with painter and fellow bohemian Charles Gill, who boasted shelves of art books. Watteau is best known for his _fêtes galantes_, depictions of rustic aristocratic revelries where erotic impulses, represented by flitting cupids, emerge from the bounteous woods or, one might prefer to say, from nature itself.

LINE 1: _Back when._ Here Nelligan launches a sentence that will rove through three idyllic stanzas to end in "far away".

LINE 2: _big black bucks._ To us, nowadays, the goat has a libidinous aspect. As a matter of fact, in Greek mythology, Dionysus took this animal's form on occasion.

LINE 7: _Skipping school._ Nelligan was a notorious truant.

LINE 10: _sons of Pan._ Goatherds. Or rather, nature spirits.

_Comments_

"Watteau Dream" is a poem of bygone country life, daubed with the poignancy of fleeting time. The poem reveals much about the poet's boyhood, or rather his re-imaginings of boyhood. In truth the poem might have been completed as late as December 1898 when Nelligan is known to have recited it at the École Littéraire.

The opening stanza, written in third person, paints a group of goatherds heading home in rustic sunset to the sound of flutes. This vision hovers in the air like a dreamy masterpiece before the eyes of the band of schoolboy truants who come romping through the countryside in stanza two. In line 8 we discover, abruptly, that the poem is being written in the first person.

Practical-minded readers might be uncomfortable with Émile's flouting of school, thinking, as did his father, how will this reprobate make a living when economic reality comes crashing down?

.../

## Watteau Dream

From the Nelligan neighborhood at the edge of the city it was easy to bolt into the countryside. "Watteau Dream" recounts for us an all-boys ramble through a space wider and freer than any school room. The truants bound through woods and falling brooks, they bivouac in stacks of hay beneath the stars. They are sons of Pan!

One of Nelligan's fundamental themes is that childhood is bliss and adulthood is decay. Time, which for Nelligan is never anything but *time passing away*, is essentially malevolent. Let's dip into mythology to see what it might mean to be a son of Pan.

Pan, who appears by name in four of Nelligan's poems, is an ancient Greek nature spirit, probably even pre-Greek, who over the ages acquired enough followers and shrines to become a god. He wasn't necessarily one of the major gods like Dionysius or Apollo, but he had staying power. In the Classical era he is a god of fields and groves, which is to say terrain at the border between civilization and wilderness. He is half human, half beast. He has the ears and horns and hind quarters of a goat. He dances and plays the panpipe. Naturally he was a favorite of shepherds and goatherds.

Pan is a lusty god, always ready to cavort with a nymph, especially in springtime. In ancient art he is often depicted with a huge erection. His list of conquests includes even the Moon, which is why she shines warmly on him as he dances in the night fields. And did I mention that he chums around with Dionysius, god of drunken orgies?

To be sure, there are some sarcastic opinions about Pan. The Cynic philosopher Diogenes of Sinope said that Pan taught shepherds how to masturbate. A sculpture unearthed in Herculaneum depicts Pan having sex with a goat. The growth of Christianity was not kind to pagan deities. We call them "pagan" because in their fading days they were disparagingly associated with the Latin *pagus*, the rural areas, the backwoods the missionaries had yet to reach. Pan was particularly frowned upon due to his carnality, and by the 4th century CE he was literally demonized. His horns, pointed ears, hooves and tail, became in Christian art the features of the Devil. But Pan survived these calumnies. He must have hidden in the woods. He re-emerged with his reed flute in European poetry in the 18th and 19th centuries, a mascot for the Romantic Movement that hankered to go back to nature. But he was a changed man-goat now, a more celebratory man-goat, with a purpose in life, which was to represent irrepressible nature.

This is the strain of Pan that Nelligan taps into. He does not bring Pan's carnal character to the fore, but rather presents him as a boyish spirit, embodying the idea of resistance to adulthood, the idea of living in a Neverland outside of time.

Incidentally, the portrayal of Pan as woodwind-playing fairy-god eventually made him eminently suitable for children, early in the 20th century, in the form of Peter Pan. Author J. M. Barrie explicitly borrowed from the Pan tradition to create his Peter Pan character, and went a step further by placing Peter in a magical land at the head of a gang of Lost Boys who refuse to grow up. That doesn't sound far distant in spirit from the picture Nelligan paints in the sunny second stanza of "Watteau Dream".

~ ~ ~

# 3. Autumn Tarantella

Do you see yon where the cattle graze,
Where leaves fall down in the valley ways,
    In the valley ways?

On the slope of my years do you see how
My faded illusions have fallen now,
    All fallen now?

How swiftly blows the raging gale,
So like the heartaches we bewail,
    That I bewail!

Do you see yon where the cattle graze,
Where leaves fall down in the valley ways,
    In the valley ways?

My autumn song will very soon
Lift my lament up to the moon,
    To the bright moon.

How swiftly blows the raging gale,
So like the heartaches we bewail,
    That I bewail!

The doggy frolics in the vale
Let us go too along that trail,
    That gloomy trail!

My autumn song will very soon
Lift my lament up to the moon,
    To the bright moon.

Summer's end the trees will mark
By shedding leaves and old dead bark,
    Their old dead bark.

Ah! See on the slope of my years how
My faded illusions have fallen now,
    All fallen now!

Notes

LINE 1: *Do you see.* The French is *vois-tu*, suggesting the poet is speaking to someone familiar to him.

Comments

The poet is wandering with his damsel in a bucolic setting, his head filled with melancholy thoughts. Falling leaves remind him of faded hopes. A date with Nelligan, if this poem is an indication, was liable to take a gloomy turn.

Émile's acquaintances named melancholy his obvious trait. Some thought that he consciously cultivated his melancholy and put it on show. In his verses he obsessively revisits melancholy topics: funerals, lost youth, suicide, and more. He pushed himself in that direction, perhaps because some core condition demanded so.

Autumn has a prominent place in Nelligan's imagination. "How Sad is October" (poem 7) and "October Roses" (poem 27) are other examples. He would die in autumn of 1941.

~ ~ ~

## 4. First Remorse

Back in the day, I dressed for school in velour neat,
While past my neck flowed curls I never cared to prune.
With eyes huge and pure like the light of the moon,
At dawn I'd depart, sack on my back, dragging my feet.

No sooner en route than some detour I'd make,
Disdaining the tattlers among my school chums,
Scaling great heights in quest of apples and plums
In the orchards that bloomed by the lanes I would take.

For a whole month I embraced this truant regime,
Far from the classroom, living by whim and by dream,
Until one nervous night when home I came at last:

My mother, her lips pressed to a crucifix held fast,
Was drowning in tears!... O how sorely I was pained!
Since that time, first in class I have ever remained.

## Notes

LINE 14: *first in class*. Poetic license, or wishful thinking. Nelligan's remorse for his failure to be a diligent student to please his excessively devout mom feels genuine, but the fact is that his marks stayed poor right to the end of his school days.

## Comments

School was a long-standing problem for Émile. His repeated absences have prompted some biographers to suggest in Nelligan's defence that he was of frail health, and therefore unable to attend. But here in "First Remorse" we discover that deliberate truancy is part of Nelligan's educational spectrum. The poem is largely buoyant and pastoral, the poet romping like Pan with a troop of fellow truants.

School cannot have been a comfortable environment for Émile. His marks were poor, he changed schools a few times, he had to repeat courses. In some courses he was two years older than his classmates.

Nelligan's most notorious unexplained absence commenced in 1895 when he was age 15. He was a no-show at the start the school year in September at the Jesuit-run Collège Sainte-Marie, and not until March 1896 did he finally make it to class. One hypothesis is that Émile was dallying with someone — we'll call her the Shepherdess, because she's the subject of "Shepherdess" (poem 5). What is clear is that, after six months God-knows-where, he returns to the world with a full-blown commitment to poetry. From June 1896 his first published poems started to appear in *Le Samedi*.

Émile officially dropped out of school in March 1897. He was, after all, engaged in his own project. He was going to be a poet, a famous poet.

~ ~ ~

# 5. Shepherdess

You that under the hollies I did love
In bucolic frolic at end of day,
Shepherdess, in the country way.
Do you recall those nights of love?
You were my star in the sky above,
My golden light where the hollies sway.

In bucolic frolic at end of day,
Under the hollies we did love,
Shepherdess, in the country way.
Where are you since those nights of love?
You are the void in the sky above,
The sorrow where the hollies sway.

## Notes

LINE 2: *bucolic frolic at end of day*. Nelligan says, *soirs de bohème champêtre,* but to translate that as "nights of rustic la Bohème" might not be helpful. The poetic notion of *la bohème* was that of the carefree pastoral life you'd gambol into, if you could, to escape industrial mankind. It was a style of life rightly or wrongly attributed to the gypsies and peasants of Bohemia in Central Europe. Eventually *la bohème* was adapted as a possibility of city life too, an ethos of living day-to-day, impecunious but loving and free.

LINE 3: *in the country way*. Nelligan says *à la mode champêtre*. Implying, therefore, that the love was carnal. In *Hamlet*, Act 3, Scene 2, Hamlet says to Ophelia: "Do you think I meant country matters?"

LINE 5: *You were my star in the sky above*. The planet Venus, in times past known as "the shepherd's star", may be what Nelligan has in mind.

## Comments

Though one of Nelligan's briefer poems, "Shepherdess" exhibits a common pattern of his poetry, starting on a high note, ending low. The first stanza recounts a time of tender love, the second finds the poet gazing into darkness and asking, What has become of you? The poem is a memory of an affair with the Shepherdess. Some critics consider her Nelligan's fantasy girl, a stock character snatched from pastoral poetry.

Formally, the poem is a *virelai*, a virelay, rooted in medieval French poetry like Nelligan's other favorite fixed forms. Though typically short, the virelay is flexible as to number and length of stanzas; each stanza is restricted to two rhymes variably arranged. In "Shepherdess" the rhyme scheme in the translation is ABBAAB for the first stanza, BABAAB for the second. The original is ABBABA BABABA.

.../

33

Shepherdess

Granted that the Shepherdess of this poem is a conventional symbol of pastoral life, might she not also be the symbol for some unknown real person? Pierre Lemieux (*Nell. am.*) argues that the Shepherdess was real and she was Nelligan's first love. If you line up the Nelligan poems in a certain way, they can be made to tell a story: it is summer of 1895 and Émile is wandering on Mount Royal, which at this time is at the northern edge of urban development; beyond the mountain lie woods, fields, and scattered villages. Émile encounters a young lady somewhere in this fringe area. Surely she is not a shepherdess, but in some way she represents rustic or 'natural' life. By late summer or early autumn, the two are meeting regularly. The poet celebrates a memory of that period in simple words in the opening lines of this poem. Love-making is implied.

Other poems in Nelligan's inventory continue the tale. In "Rural Chateau" the poet imagines living with his pastoral maiden in a country house. They visit a chapel adorned with chrysanthemums in "Chapel in the Woods". But matters take a sad turn and in "The Dead Girl's Slipper" the poet clutches a memento she left behind in his room, a slipper "with buckles of fragrant silk, like a mysterious drug held in my hands". He tells us in that poem that his beloved has departed:

To sleep forever beneath the pine
Along the cold and mournful path.

Nelligan alludes to the girl's death and funeral in several other poems including "How Sad is October" (poem 7) and "La Sorella dell' Amore" (poem 15).

Lemieux's account grounds Nelligan's persistent melancholy and depression in this personal romantic tragedy. Writer André Vanasse (*Nell. spasme*) gives this girl the name "Ilse", gracing her with Swiss-German (quasi-Bohemian!) roots.

The Ilse concept explains a lot. Above all, what was Nelligan up to between September 1895 and March 1896, when he should have been at school but wasn't? Was he dallying with Ilse, as Lemieux thinks, and was he decimated by her loss?

Ilse provides plausible kindling for the sense of guilt that, as we shall see, eventually crushes Nelligan. Her story entails the sin of sex outside of wedlock, and then the cruel fate of her soul being summoned to Judgment with that stain on her account. We might find these considerations appallingly superstitious now, but they were part of Nelligan's religious formation.

On the other hand, shepherdesses such as Ilse were easy to concoct, they had populated pastoral poetry since time immemorial, capering amidst fields and flowers and running brooks, auguring simple and sincere love. To lose Ilse would be a heartbreaker, but for Romantic poets a background of heartbreak was *de rigueur*. A deceased Ilse would fit right in with Nelligan's poetic purposes.

What we *do* know is that Nelligan fell out of sight for several months and had some sort of experience because when he returned he was writing poetry such as "Shepherdess".

~ ~ ~

## 6. Villanelle Violin

In the valley breeze where the moonlight glows
Come all ye blonde belles and brown-haired beaus,
Where the fiddle plays and the woodwind blows,
    Dance the villanelle!

Sweet perfumes the fields on you bestow,
Come kindle your joy in the bonfire's glow;
Be merry about it, by leaps and bounds go,
    Dance the villanelle!

The old folks are here, on an oaken seat,
With tears in their eyes, they mark every beat
As you brush right past on your joyful feet...
    Dance the villanelle!

Go to it gaily! May the moon shine bright,
Let it paint your brows with its shimmering light;
This feast of Saint Jean, dance into the night,
    Dance the villanelle!

## Notes

TITLE: A villanelle violin is one that is played at a villanelle, a country dance.

LINE 15: *feast of Saint Jean.* In 1834 the Catholic feast day of Saint-Jean-Baptiste, June 24, became the national holiday for Lower Canada and it has remained so for the successor state, Québec. The Saint-Jean is a festive, celebratory event; Nelligan here captures the rural hoedown aspect.

## Comments

You can hear the music in this remarkable poem — it moves briskly like the swirling dancers. When the young folk brush past the teary old folks, the tune continues but with an overtone of melancholy and irony that impacts one's appreciation of the poem as a whole.

Émile spent most of his days in Montréal, but he was familiar too with the rural ambience that buoys this poem. He had only to walk to the north side of Mount Royal to find an agrarian world. For several years the Nelligan family summered at Cacouna, a resort town on the lower St. Lawrence River surrounded by farmland.

~ ~ ~

## 7. How Sad is October

How sad is October with its indigo sigh
    When evening is nigh!

Its funereal air so lovingly clings
    To morose things.

In a chamber rose and white a maiden white and rose
    Takes repose.

All the village is hushed. The shepherds, home at last,
    Think of the past

When beside the singing brooks along the trails
    Through hills and dales

She ran along with them. Angel of the field,
    O memory sealed

Of youth forever sweet. But Fritz the goatherd
    Says not a word.

This grand old man, king of the goats that gambol free
    Beside the sea,

Loved her. Better had he hated! He was her shield
    That would not yield,

That was unscathed by Time's abrasive tide.
    But when she died

This big-hearted old guy cried his eyes out and then
    Needed two men

To hold his arms and guide him into the chapel.
    A shovel

Prepares a place of exile from this life of pain
    In the sub-terrain.

That path I too follow. In the ground she lies prone
    All alone

I hear her in my dreams. She's in the bells that chime
    At evening time

A brotherly memory of her I hold near,
    A struggle dear

With the devil of old. For me this pain's not new,
    I'm scorched right through

From its fiery ovens that keep me burning,
    In embers turning.

Pain from such thirst that I could drink whole worlds with ease
    And all of their seas.

Pain where like a lily on a shelf I wither away,
    With no words to say…

How sad is October with its indigo sigh
    When evening is nigh!

How Sad is October

<u>Notes</u>

LINE 2: *evening*. Nelligan says *La Vesprée*, which is when the bells chime for evening prayer.

LINE 11: *Angel of the field*. Nelligan says *archange bucolique*, bucolic archangel. She may be an iteration of the Shepherdess; see the Comments to "Shepherdess" (poem 5).

LINE 13: *Fritz the goatherd*. This Fritz appears also in another Nelligan poem, *Pan Moderne,* where he is a hundred-year-old flute-playing goatherd who dies chaste, penniless, and wise — taking the pastoral lifestyle with him, therefore, as the century ends.

LINE 17: *Loved her.* If this is indeed the same Fritz as in *Pan Moderne*, this love must be avuncular.

LINE 33: *the devil of old*. Nelligan says, *l'autre d'antan*, which would be "someone from the old days". The suddenly infernal environment in the next few lines supports a diabolist interpretation. Nelligan frequently describes demons as being age-old.

<u>Comments</u>

This is a poem where the lyrics can carry you along, but in terms of meaning it seems a ramble. Here are the plot points of the story Nelligan is telling:

> October is sad
> A maiden sleeps
> The village is hushed
> The shepherds remember the girl
> Old Fritz cried when she died
> A shovel digs her grave
> I too must die
> She is in my dreams
> The relationship was brotherly
> I fought a devil
> I'm burning inside
> October is sad

Approximately the first half of the poem portrays the autumnal sorrow of country people — Fritz, the shepherds, and the villagers — over the loss of the pastoral girl. She may be an instance of the Shepherdess who appears in several Nelligan poems. See "Shepherdess" (poem 5). She also stands for pastoralism. Fritz is a sort of Pan who protects the girl, or as is painfully obvious now, is unable to protect her. The girl dies from unspecified cause and Fritz collapses in grief.

Suddenly the poet discloses that he was involved in some struggle concerning this maiden. He cannot mean a struggle against old Fritz, a pathetic figure left behind. More likely the poet's struggle has been with the devil that urged him to be less brotherly with the pastoral girl. We don't know exactly how that turned out. A social factor in those days was that the question of sin meant that sex could be spoken of only in indirect, even evasive, fashion. What we do know is that this poem ends on a note that sounds like a poet ripping his heart out.

~ ~ ~

## 8. Red Aubade

Sunrise splatters the hills with red
    Where a fine-spun mist hangs about,

And you hear an ox groaning with dread
    And steam puffing out from its snout.

The butchering hour now draws nigh.
    Holding the beast by its halter,

Pulling their neckerchiefs way up high,
    The workers prepare for the slaughter.

The ax with such a chuff does strike,
    For once the men are in silent mood.

*Procumbit bos.* And elephant-like
    The beast crumbles in solitude.

Blood spurts. The beast plows with his horns
    The earth that is stained a ghastly hue,

As with bellowing chant Phoebus mourns
    The ox that was broken in two.

<u>Notes</u>

TITLE: An aubade is a morning song, traditionally for parting lovers, but Nelligan has a different sort of parting in mind.

LINE 11: *Procumbit bos.* This allusion in Latin is to Virgil, Book 5 of the *Aenead*. A boxer strikes an ox square between its horns, whereupon *procumbit humi bos*, "the ox falls to the ground". Though he had been a fitful student, Nelligan performed relatively well in language courses. Virgil would surely have been among his readings in Latin.

LINE 15: *Phoebus.* The god known as Phoebus Apollo, who is the Sun, here mourning a loss of life.

<u>Comments:</u>

The poet in his perambulations happens upon a slaughterhouse in the reddening morning light and what follows is a vignette about the ignoble death of a mighty animal at the hands of industrial civilization.

Mythology was abundant in 19th-century poetry, but Nelligan's use of it here is not merely decorative. To his mind it's the only recourse for a burning question: Who above us will acknowledge the crime of this frightful destiny, the tragedy of being in the world?

The prevailing religion seems not to give adequate answer, for, as in the later "Nocturnal Confession", which in a sense is his own personal execution poem Nelligan does not expect a reply from an abstract universal God. Instead he looks to the ancient animistic sky filled with divinities who inhabit the same atmosphere as us. Nelligan has made the right choice, since he obtains a godly emotional response: Apollo the sun god, also held to be lord of music and poetry, lets out a cry that quakes across the sky.

~ ~ ~

## 9. Monks in File

They move in file along the corridors antique,
Heads bowed, tolling their prayers on enormous chaplets;
A purplish splendor fills the space as the sun sets
With blood-red rays that play upon the stones monastic.

Already vespers hour has poured a flame ecstatic
Into their swollen hearts where simmer the secrets
Of their worldly disdain, of their mournful regrets,
Of all the suppressed urges of their flesh cenobitic.

They march in the dark and nothing troubles them at all,
Not even the hideous fiery shadows that crawl
Along the wall behind them to the chapel door,

Not even calls from the devil down below,
Supreme Tempter that bids the rebel passions grow
Inside these silent ghosts of Jesus Christ.

## Notes

LINE 2: *chaplets*. Strings of beads, like rosaries, used for counting off one's mandatory repetitive prayers — apparently in this monastery the strings are long.

## Comments

This sonnet, dated June 1897, was one of five Nelligan poems that ran in the weekly *Le Monde illustré* that year. Nelligan was 17 years old. The play of light and shadow, and the sardonic outcome, attest to a surprising poetic maturity on his part. The monks are on the surface holy and serene but at the same time they are monads enswathed in self-deception as sub-surface sexual urges make claim on them.

Nelligan composed several poems about members of religious orders including monks, nuns, and priests. This circumstance is sometimes cited in the charge that Nelligan's editor Louis Dantin, who actually did belong to the clerical milieu, secretly composed the poems.

But again, Nelligan was raised in a thoroughly Catholic environment where religious orders were ubiquitous. His parents were devout. One of the schools he attended from age 13 to 15, le Collège de Montréal, specialized in teaching candidates for the priesthood. Nelligan would surely have mooted the possibility of a religious vocation for himself. In "Monks in File" he gives himself good reason to reject the idea, on the basis of the sexual self-repression required. He concludes that this would be a path of suffering — Christ in this vignette is Sufferer, not Redeemer.

There is a separate version of this poem that comes with a happy ending (heavenly light pours down upon the persevering monks) that Dantin managed to gather from Nelligan's notes. It could be that Dantin sidestepped the version that had originally appeared in *Le Monde illustré* in an effort to avoid offending broader religious sensibilities, not necessarily just those of Madame Nelligan.

~ ~ ~

## 10. Wild Country

The trees like a rabble of rickety old guys,
Their limbs twisted in mimes of writhing despair,
Stretch over the hills to the faraway skies
Like some march of the damned with grim torments to bear.

It's Winter, it's Death; where the arctic snow lies,
The hunters, freezing in spite of the furs they wear,
Eyes fixed on the distance where flames of campfires rise,
Lay the whip on their horses, the faster to get there.

The wind howls, hail slashes down; night falls, all is dark;
And then of a sudden, prowling in shadows stark,
A ferocious pack of famished wolves appears;

They bound through the woods, this teeming savage race,
And their wild fiery eyes stoking your deepest fears
Send golden sparks flying through this bare lonely space.

## Notes

LINE 5: *arctic snow*. Nelligan never saw the Arctic, but he and his poet buddy Arthur de Bussières in early 1898 formed a plan to pan for gold in the Klondike gold rush. The dream was short-lived since they hadn't two cents to rub together for a train to the West. Then de Bussières fell ill and the project was forgotten.

## Comments

"Wild Country" was submitted in May 1897 to *Le Monde illustré* and was published in August of that year. Along with "Monks in File" (poem 9), it represents Nelligan at a Parnassian peak of sorts, exhibiting rigorous form and a calm detachment, as if keeping himself out of the picture.

At the same time, Nelligan manages to turn the "arctic" into a sort of hellscape. The trees are writhing, the animals are oppressed, the hunters flail in despair. Winter, Nelligan says explicitly, stands for Death. Wolves with fiery eyes are ready to pounce.

Thus Nelligan the Symbolist comes to the fore. The landscape and animals are hardly an objective presentation; rather, they are designed as symbols of a state of mind, even as symbols of a truth about being in the world.

~ ~ ~

## 11. Two Portraits of my Mother

My mother, how I love her in this painting made
In her glory days when she was a maiden fair;
With her brow the color of lilies, and eyes that flare,
She glowed like a mirror in a golden frame inlaid.

But look, this second picture shows a later phase
Where furrows line the precious marble of her face;
Time has erased her girlish shine without a trace
Since her bridal hymn sounded in her rose-poem days.

Sorrow consumes me when these portraits I compare:
One brow is bright with joy, the other grim with care;
A golden sun there was, and then the fog sets down.

So here's a puzzle that our guarded hearts hold deep:
How is it that I smile to see that worried frown?
And the picture where she smiles, how is it that I weep?

_Comments_

An unbearably sad poem. The poet's mother, young, then old. The tragedy of the passage of time. Then comes that poignant fillip at the end, the inversion of frown and smile.

So inconsolable is this poem that one might think the poet's mother had died. In fact, when Émile wrote this poem in 1897, Madame Nelligan was very much alive, running a household with three kids.

Émile wrote several poems expressly about her. And she is implicit, I would think, in many more.

She was born Émilie Amanda Hudon in 1856, in Kamouraska, on the banks of the St. Lawrence as it widens toward Gaspésie. She married David Nelligan, Émile's father, in Rimouski in 1875 when she was 19 and he 26.

It was from her that Émile derived his artistic nature. Madame Nelligan was an amateur pianist. She kept in practice at home and was diligent to take young Émile to high-level concerts such as the celebrated visit to Montréal of pianist Ignace Paderewski in April 1896. Émile went on to compose a number of poems such as "Funeral Marches" (poem 14) that recalled the Chopin sonata Paderewski played that night.

~ ~ ~

## 12. Moonlight of the Mind

My thought is the color of strange gleams from afar
From some sea-bottom crypt at a depth never seen.
It glitters at times with sparks of esoteric green
Deep where rays of the sun strike a void black as tar.

Amid sighing fountains in gardens without par,
It has known soft evenings and fragrances keen;
My thought is the color of strange gleams from afar
From some sea-bottom crypt at a depth never seen.

It forever pays court to its ladylove star,
In the angelic land where its passions convene,
And far from this physical world so ugly and mean,
It longs to soar where celestial cities are.

My thought is the color of golden moons afar.

<u>Notes</u>

TITLE: The French title *Clair de lune intellectuelle* strictly speaking means "Intellectual Moonlight".

LINE 12: *celestial cities.* Nelligan writes *célestes Athènes*, celestial Athens, combining a Christian notion of Heaven with a Parnassian fondness for the locales of classical culture.

<u>Comments</u>

Louis Dantin chose to place "Moonlight of the Mind" at the head of his 1904 compilation of Nelligan's poetry, perhaps supposing that the book should start off with an artistic statement. But this poem is more a sensory display than a declaration of principles.

What is the poet telling us about his mind? That it consists of sub-surface pyrotechnics. That it is soaked in a sense-memory of Eden (the garden with the fountains). That it longs to take flight and leave our miserable world behind.

The poem finishes on an aspirational note, in a glow of golden moons. "Gold" and "golden" are among Nelligan's favorite images. Gold is perfection, the epitome of what can be valued in this world.

"Moonlight of the Mind" is a rondel, albeit a pensive one thanks to Nelligan's 12-syllable lines. Compare this to "Rondel to My Pipe" (poem 30) with its impulsive 8-syllable lines.

~ ~ ~

# 13. Old Streets

To you what do the old streets say
    In the olden town
Coated with dust from long decay,
    Slowly crumbling down,
Dreaming of things long passed away,
To you what do the old streets say?

When late at night you pass this way
    Paying them respect,
"There's more than one guy old and grey
    Whose soul we do reflect,"
Is what in the fog the old streets say
When late at night you pass this way.

"Like all who in the night have plied
    Down our ancient ways
Bearing darkened urns inside
    From their impure days,
That's how Remorse does slink and hide
Like all who in the night have plied."

These ancient pavements that you tread,
    That is what they say,
Where age-old dusty layers spread
    From the long decay
Of all your glories passed away,
O cities sad and dead!

## Comments

Poems such as this that emphasize the grimy, sordid city, are the urban flipside of the pastoral coin. City life represents a fall from pastoral bliss, a misdirection from youthful innocence.

The decaying streets speak in a knowing voice to the wanderer in the fog. They've seen this type of derelict before. The revelation comes in the third stanza: the wanderer carries a darkened urn inside. This passage is fodder for the argument that Nelligan bore within himself some secret sin, as exhibited later in "Nocturnal Confession" (poem 44).

Nelligan was himself a habitual wanderer of the city. Vieux Montréal and the old port were often on his itinerary. There were times when his wanderings were forced, when he was avoiding turmoil at home, for instance.

~ ~ ~

## 14. Funeral Marches

Within me I hear voices funereal
Clamoring transcendentally,
As a German motif musically
Propels these marches proverbial.

Amidst mad shudders vertebral
If I sob uncontrollably,
It's because I hear voices funereal
Clamoring transcendentally.

Like a herd of zebras spectral
My dream roams bizarrely;
I'm haunted so entirely
That in my darkness personal

I hear moans of voices funereal.

## Notes

LINE 3: *a German motif.* Nelligan may be alluding to Chopin's *Sonata #2*, influenced by Bach and Beethoven.

## Comments

This rondel is one of several Nelligan poems directly or indirectly pointing to the composer Frederic Chopin. Émile in general was highly susceptible to music. From an early age he had heard his mother playing the great composers at her piano.

Chopin's Piano Sonata #2 in particular made a deep impression on him. The piece contains a magnificent *marche funèbre*, or funeral march, whose fearsome initial notes have become a musical cliché signifying death. When Nelligan heard the selection performed by the illustrious Paderewski in 1896, the music was still new and powerful. Nelligan was haunted by its dark tones. Chopin's funeral march makes death seem magisterial and spellbinding. Graves and graveyards are frequent images in Nelligan's work. Several of his poems express death wishes.

In "Funeral Marches" the poet is saying that when he hears funeral marches, he hears death calling from within himself. He speaks as if Death were a force inside him, even a guide. Suicide will soon enough be in his thoughts.

~ ~ ~

# 15. La Sorella dell' Amore

Death, tell us what you do with your prizes so fine,
The virgins that our fires upon your altars burn?
Answer, when shall we immortal be, to sojourn
In the luminescence of your Alpines divine?

I've lived the Ideal. That fairyland was mine
When she was here…I don't know, I did discern
Great castles rising in her eyes when night did turn,
Massifs of pride enwrapped by woods and groves benign.

My dear, it's evening; come, through the woods we will go,
We'll follow together the road that's rough and crude
That runs past the chapel of old, the one you know.

I call to you, sister! But silence you exude.
Lucille died yesterday, and today my sobs flow
Like a useless bell that tolls in solitude.

## Notes

TITLE: The title is identical in English and French, *La Sorella dell' Amore* being Italian for, literally, "The Sister of Love".

LINE 4: *Alpines divine.* Nelligan says *célestes Riphées*, referring to the mythical Riphean Mountains the classical Greeks placed in a vague and frozen northern land's-end.

LINE 13: *Lucille died yesterday.* Nelligan did not have a sister named Lucille either deceased or alive. Lucille may be some unknown sisterly friend, or an invention. Nelligan's real sisters, Gertrude and Éva, were alive and in their mid-teens at the time this poem was composed. Years later, after Gertrude's death from breast cancer in 1925, Éva created a new version of the poem, substituting "Gertrude" for the original "Lucille". Nelligan was in the asylum at the time. Perhaps displaying the revised poem was Éva's way of giving Émile presence at Gertrude's funeral.

## Comments

Time's ultimate sorrow is death, which is where many of Nelligan's poems lead, expressly or otherwise. This poem addresses Death directly by name. Why are the innocent sacrificed, the poet demands to know. He seems to ridicule the idea of Heaven.

It's as if Death were an evil god, actively snatching people away, including in this poem the heaven-on-earth lass with the Romantic eyes the poet peers into. The awesome cliffs and castles he sees in her eyes were staple fare in the Romantic era. The poet calls upon his sister of love to stroll with him back to an era of simple faith, symbolized by a country chapel. But she's not answering. The poet, I surmise, is standing at her graveside. From the chapel a lonely bell chimes.

Pierre Lemieux (*Nell. am.*) contends that Lucille — the sole occurrence of this name in Nelligan's poetry — is a reprise of the Shepherdess (see poem 5), Nelligan's pastoral sweetheart prematurely stolen from life.

~ ~ ~

## 16. Placet

My queen, do you consent this buckle to unclose,
That of your wavy hair my scissors might one curl snip,
That some tiny breath of birdsong I might sip
And from your pearly eyes a night of love suppose?

In the glade of my heart, like a blackbird's pip,
The music of your soul like a reed flute flows.
My queen, do you consent this buckle to unclose,
That of your wavy hair my scissors might one curl snip?

Flower of silk with scents of lily, berle, and rose,
I'll give it back to you, our secret will not slip.
Let that be in Eden, the day when we take ship
Upon a perfect sea where no storm ever blows.

My queen, do you consent this buckle to unclose?

_Notes_

TITLE: Nelligan is deploying a quaint word from the great medieval days of monarchies. _Placet_ derives from the Latin verb _placere_ ("to please"). The royal personage's _placet_ meant: it pleases me, therefore let it be so. The word also came to be used as the name for the petition one might submit in hope of winning the monarch's favor.

LINE 4: _your pearly eyes._ If this poem is addressed to the Nelligan love interest known as Gretchen, it may be relevant that the name Gretchen stems from the Greek word _margarites_ meaning "little pearl".

LINE 10: _I'll give it back to you._ Give what back? Your flower.


_Comments_

This rondel, plausibly belonging to 1898, is head-over-heels for a newfound love, maybe the mysterious Gretchen. The characterization is sensual, distinguishing her from the poet's other love interests such as the chaste Saint Cecilia (see poem 24) and the mostly off-stage Shepherdess (see poem 5).

The quest for the curl traditionally symbolizes the determination to become intimate with the adored one.

French symbolist poet Stéphane Mallarmé (1842-1898) once composed a wry _Placet futile_ addressed to a princess, asking her to appoint him shepherd of her smiles. Nelligan's earnest "Placet" makes the adored one a queen and cajoles her for a lock of hair.

I choose to take "Placet" as a rare thing in Nelligan, an optimistic poem. He and his love will embark on a trouble-free sea. She has only to say yes. Did Nelligan present this poem to Gretchen as a proposal? People sent each other notes in those pre-telephone days. A poet in love would naturally send a poem. He might have presented it in person — on her doorstep, say.

The ship of life that sails upon a perfect sea in the final lines of this poem will be replaced in a year or so with the shipwreck of "The Ship of Gold" (poem 45).

~ ~ ~

## 17. A Portrait of Dante

That's him, the pilgrim from the shadow-land returned,
His features darkened from the raging fires of Hell,
Yet his eyes swim with sublime visions, you can tell,
This peerless artist by his own city spurned.

Jealous rogues hounded him, but he riposted well,
Laying bare their sick crimes; then far from them he turned,
High in Olympian mountains he went to dwell,
And the peace of a clean heart was the prize he earned.

O Dante Alighieri, guardian of the tomb,
Upon the wall of sages your lofty works will loom,
Emblazoned for all time, indelible and proud!

Through time as vast as God your fame will be relayed,
Since eternal Heaven and Hell are now endowed
With the music of your verses that never will fade.

## Notes

TITLE: The subject is Alighieri Dante (1265-1321), famed Italian poet.

LINE 5: *Jealous rogues hounded him.* Dante was exiled from Florence in 1302 when an inimical political faction won control of the city. During his exile in Verona and elsewhere, he composed his masterpiece *Divine Comedy*. When Florence later tried to reclaim him by offering an amnesty, he turned it down.

LINE 9: *guardian of the tomb.* Nelligan was presumably captivated by Dante's poetic peregrinations through Hell, Purgatory, and Paradise in the *Divine Comedy*.

## Comments

"A Portrait of Dante" is one of Émile's hero-worship poems. For Émile, Dante is a persecuted genius who has seen Heaven and Hell and who has triumphed through his timeless art. Nelligan also wrote poetic eulogies for two other of his dead heroes, poet Charles Baudelaire and composer Frederic Chopin.

In a *poème-portrait*, a portrait poem, the poet's task was to paint his subject in words. Hence the initial focus on Dante's facial features. In fact, Nelligan is painting a portrait of a portrait, for we know thanks to his friend Charles Gill that for this poem Nelligan was contemplating a *sanguine* of Dante, a sketch in red chalk or pastel on paper.

The poem was first published in *Le Monde illustré* in May 1898. A more refined copy came to light a few years later — Nelligan had given it to Charles Gill — and it is this version, which finally landed in *Le Nationaliste* magazine in March 1904, that I translate here.

~ ~ ~

# 18. Correggio's Last Angel

In his Italian garret lying,
Eyes haggard, cheeks pallid, yet
Strong of heart and without regret,
The divine Correggio was dying.

Gathered round the dreadful sickbed
The master's children and good wife
Try to impart some of their life
Into his heart already near-dead.

But some vision lodged in his mind
Fuels his body's fever and sweat;
The groans that shake his soul beget
Pulsations of the oddest kind.

He wants to paint! He starts to climb
Slowly from his pillow, up a ways
Like some archangel in a daze
Forgetting Heaven for a time.

His eye scanning the family lair
Suddenly stops, wholly beguiled
To find his model waiting there
In the cradle of his newborn child.

Right by the easel the child lay,
Pink of face, wrapped in orange shawl,
With tiny hands joined as if to pray
To the Baby Jesus picture on the wall.

His son's prayer, would you believe,
Summons Eden back into sight:
On this golden Italian eve,
A vision of purest light.

Someone bring me a brush, and fast!
My colors! the old artist cries,
While my child in the cradle lies,
Catch his sad pose before it's past.

My brush! the master raves once more,
I want to capture on the fly
This white as snow ideal before
It dissolves in the golden sky.

How he paints! How he unbars
His genius in sweeps of the arm
To portray this fair cherub's charm
In a chemise as bright as stars.

But the painter, suddenly beset
With gagging throat, falls down. He dies.
Upon his neck the beaded sweat
Into pearls of wax quickly dries.

And thus the artist's life was done,
His heart sworn to art right to the last;
He made an angel of his son,
Then made an orphan of him fast.

## Correggio's Last Angel

### Notes

TITLE: Italian artist Antonio Allegri da Correggio, a master painter of the High Italian Renaissance, was known for such works as *Jupiter and Io* and *Assumption of the Virgin*. He was born in 1489 in Correggio, about 25 kilometers from Parma, and died there in 1534.

LINE 24: *Baby Jesus*. Nelligan says *le Bambino*.

### Comments

"Correggio's Last Angel" appeared in *La Patrie* on October 22, 1898, which was the plump (16-page) Saturday edition. It was a longish poem, but the strong rhythm held the readers' attention once their eyes fell upon it in the midst of page 11, seven cacophonous columns wide, packed with news stories alongside steamship and railroad advertisements.

The poem consists of a dozen stanzas, all of them quatrains (four-liners). Some of them, such as stanza one in this translation, employ "enclosed rhyme" which follows the pattern ABBA, where the A-rhymes 'enclose' the B-rhymes. Others such as stanza five have "alternate rhyme" following the pattern CDCD. Nelligan meticulously furnishes his poem with exactly six ABBA and six CDCD stanzas.

Nelligan's advent in *La Patrie* owes much to the influence of Robertine Barry (1863-1910), famous in her own right as a pioneer in female journalism in Canada. Robertine wrote columns and managed a popular section of *La Patrie* with a marked interest in literature. She regularly held salons; young Nelligan, son of her friend Émilie, began attending and reciting his poems. Robertine became a strong supporter of his poetry. *La Patrie* published several more Nelligan poems subsequent to "Correggio's Last Angel". After the poet's internment in 1899, the paper helped keep his name alive, as late as 1937 sending a journalist to report on the poet's continued existence at Saint-Jean-de-Dieu hospital.

"Correggio's Last Angel" belongs to what has been dubbed Nelligan's Italian phase. In that category see also, "A Portrait of Dante" (poem 17). Renaissance Italy was exotic with its free-wheeling cities and its inspired artists. Nelligan was so enchanted by the milieu that he made a start on learning to speak Italian.

No doubt Nelligan was roused by the idea that Correggio to his last breath was devoted fanatically to his art. Or rather was devoted to something beyond art, to a vision of purest light.

Note the bitter irony at the end: the angelic child immortalized in art will in reality live an orphan's life.

~ ~ ~

## 19. Sonnet of Gold

This triumphal evening, how poorly frost will fare
As the divine quivers of spring come surging high:
Winter is gone! Bravo! Let April keep its eye
On the floral seraglio entrusted to its care.

Throw open the shutters, imbibe the bracing air
Imbued with reflections of rosy pristine sky,
Let it fill the boudoir where we love, you and I,
In the slackening notes of the lute you play there.

Allegro, Yvette, allegro, believe you me,
Not sipping tea while you tap your piano here
But drunk on golden birdsong is where I'd rather be.

Let's wander in the verdant park and you will find,
On this glorious eve, that it's perfectly clear
That spring is worth all of Handel and Mozart combined.

## Notes

LINE 8: *lute*. The lute is curvaceous, fundamentally erotic. It is the instrument *par excellence* of medieval minstrels and lyrical poetry.

LINE 9: *Allegro*. A musical term meaning quick, lively. The poet is urging Yvette to hurry.

## Comments

A happy, breezy poem belonging to spring of 1898. Love is going well. The poet wants to take his lady sauntering in the springtime park.

Pierre Lemieux (*Nell. am.*) places this poem at the head of a sequence of fifteen poems that relate to "Gretchen", one of Émile's amatory interests. Here she is called "Yvette," as Nelligan had yet to settle on a name for her, but she already shows the Gretchen traits of (1) being associated with music, and (2) not emotionally needing the poet.

The second stanza suggests there has been lute-playing and love-making. The first stanza sets it all up with nature's triumphal quivers overcoming the coldness barrier. In Nelligan's era, one had to speak indirectly about intimate matters.

Lemieux's thesis is not unanimously applauded, it must be said. After all, why not just let Yvette be Yvette? Emile Talbot (*Reading Nell.*) warns that trying to link various characters in the poems to one specific person in Nelligan's real life might lead to distortions. One would always be fitting the verses into some superimposed romantic plot.

~ ~ ~

## 20. Ecclesiastical Siesta

*A summer sketch*

Truly he looks fine in his new soutane arrayed,
This dear little abbot, plump, face shaven bright,
For whom a splendid meal is but a sinless delight ...
That's what he's dreaming of beneath the plane-tree's shade.

The noon bell rings. The sun on high does its parade
And Monsieur the vicar — O! scandalous sight! —
He lies rapt and rotund on the lawn, sleeping tight,
Dreaming of the great sins some wanton harlot made.

The kitchen help comes to see, behind the drapes they stay
Till Blanche shoos Michel, Louise, and the pooch away,
And off they skedaddle, laughing all the while.

The vicar, however, no penance will he do;
He stretches out and murmurs with an angelic smile
That Bacchus, after all, was a good Christian too.

## Notes

TITLE: While *Ecclesiastical Siesta* is a mouthful in English, the French title *Sieste ecclésiastique* slides more smoothly off the tongue.

SUBTITLE: *A summer sketch.* Summer of 1898 at the latest. Too good-humored to belong to 1899.

LINE 2: *abbot.* Nelligan says *abbé*, abbot, but the context is sarcastic. The character is a parish priest.

LINE 8: *great sins.* The insinuation would be that the priest heard these sins in the confessional.

LINE 14: *Bacchus.* Ancient Roman god of wine.

## Comments

This poem is a bit different for Nelligan. It is humor, and for his day it was irreverent.

Some of Émile's friends were anti-clerical. That was what kept this poem alive: it circulated in a sort of literary underground. When it finally saw light of day, in the anti-clerical journal *Les Débats* in January 1900, four months after Nelligan's internment, the poem generated controversy. What seems like light mockery to us seemed sacrilegious in a society where open criticism of the clergy was verboten.

Madame Nelligan was troubled that some of her son's poetry could be taken as blasphemous. There exists an amended, milder version of this poem that removes the gourmandise and the harlot from the picture. Louis Dantin preserved that tamer version in his files but couldn't bring himself to print it; he left the poem entirely out of his compilation of Nelligan's poems.

~ ~ ~

## 21. Gretchen the Pale

Her beauty is like some portrait by Rubens made,
Its serene majesty so very like her own.
Her voice like gentle song radiates a golden tone
Like mandolins from Venetian balconies played.

Fresh from the bath, her hair in glistening cascade
Curls round her virgin flesh like a cloak loosely thrown;
Her step, a creamy sigh like chiffon over stone,
Is like some cherubim passing in evening shade.

She's like strange glowing gold. Might she an angel be?
Does she from Eden come? Or from some darker place?
What is it, this masterpiece of clay so rare?

Look at her rising, bare of chest, like a sprouting tree.
Lithe Anadyomene — she's a demon, beware!
She's the Paros that kills with her marble embrace!

## Notes

TITLE: By "pale" Nelligan may be alluding to the near-white color of the Parian marble of which Gretchen, it will turn out, is metaphorically made.

LINE 1: *Rubens*. Flemish artist Peter Paul Rubens (1577-1640), known particularly for his sensual nudes. It's true that, as Louis Dantin said, Nelligan "never saw the Louvre", but the young man nevertheless had a sense of Rubens as a painter of erotic scenes. With that as a cue, Nelligan goes on to paint a portrait in verse of a woman emerging from her bath.

LINE 12: *Look at her rising*. That is, rising from the bath.

LINE 13: *Anadyomene*. This means something like "She who rises from the sea" and is one of the epithets of the Roman love goddess Venus, who, by her Greek name Aphrodite, had emerged from the frothy sea near Cyprus. She is a watery goddess, her flesh is supple and her hair flows in waves.

LINE 14: *Paros*. An Aegean island famed for its flawless white marble used for sculptures in the classical era.

## Comments

Gretchen's name appears in four of Nelligan's poems and she may be the unnamed subject of several more. She was, initially, his adored one, as in "Placet" (poem 16). From her name, she was Swiss-German, indirectly evincing a Bohemian pastoral landscape. He encountered her possibly in 1897. The Nelligan family lived on avenue Laval just north of carré St.-Louis. Some commentators speculate that Gretchen lived in the same neighborhood.

As a matter of fact, André Vanasse in his fictionalized biography, *Nelligan: le spasme de vivre*, situates Gretchen just a few doors away from the Nelligan house. He has Émile one night stand mesmerized on the sidewalk as behind half-open curtains Gretchen undresses for bed, slowly, deliberately, item by item, before she blows out the lamp. It's fiction, but the core image strikes a chord: Nelligan in thrall on the outside looking in.

.../

## Gretchen the Pale

From the poems, we gather that Gretchen is a paragon of beauty and that she is musically gifted — like Émile's mother. But she has a different look from his mother; she is more like one of the Alsatian angels that popped up in Parisian poetry now and then.

The nature of the Nelligan-Gretchen relationship is a matter of guesswork, but it looks like Gretchen ultimately spurned him. "Gretchen the Pale", which may belong to the summer of 1898, is more or less a juvenile hate poem. Yet it commences in Parnassian languor as the poet elaborates a sustained portrait of Gretchen's grace and beauty, likened to a work of art. The third stanza, the turning point, introduces a quandary: is she angel or demon? In the fourth stanza, his Gretchen/Venus is transformed into a monster whose coital hug is cold and lethal.

Some say the affair never happened, that Nelligan was too shy to approach his Gretchen, or even that he invented her out of whole cloth, a figment drawn from his readings and adolescent imagination. He likely had read French poet Théodore de Banville's poem *Sabbat*, which features a golden-haired, sapphire-eyed Gretchen flying nude over the rooftops of Paris. The name Gretchen evoked a stereotype, the way names such as Heidi and Brunhilde later would do. Paul Wyczynski (*Nell. Bio.*) says there was a sort of Gretchen craze in Montreal at this time, with the young folks dancing a "Gretchen polka". The name Gretchen is also hallowed in literature as the name of Doctor Faust's angelic girlfriend in Goethe's play *Faust*.

As Nelligan's companion, however, Gretchen is unattested. The evidence for her is entirely literary: the poems demand her presence. Pierre Lemieux (*Nell. am.*) finds fifteen poems in the Nelligan oeuvre that seem to relate to Gretchen; they trace an arc from the optimistic early days of love (see "Sonnet of Gold", poem 19), through days of disenchantment ("Robin in the Woods", poem 36), culminating in "The Ship of Gold" (poem 45) where she is remembered as a Siren.

Personally, I'm inclined to believe that Nelligan's Gretchen was a real person, and that the relationship between the pair reached a physical stage before it ended. Granted that artistic work can stretch one's imagination, it nevertheless seems far-fetched to suppose that Émile dreamed the girl up, then dreamed up a rejection, all so he could write deeply bitter verse about her.

Note the mostly autodidact erudition on display as Nelligan constructs an antique patina for this poem. Rubens is a Renaissance master. Venice likewise recalls that era. Paros recalls classical Greece. And Eden, of course, is as far back as one can travel.

Outside of the title, Nelligan does not use Gretchen's name in this poem, but rather refers to her as *Anadyomène*. Venus Anadyomene is the subject of well-known paintings by Botticelli, Titian, Ingres, and others, typically displaying Venus on her half-shell riding on the ocean foam. Nelligan might have known de Banville's poem *L'invincible* wherein the poet drinks to forget a lost love only to have the "invincible Anadyomene" appear in his wine glass.

Gretchen was Nelligan's Venus who, like de Banville's Venus, would return to haunt the poet in dark days ahead.

~ ~ ~

## 22. Brother Alfus, Part I

A chaste man was he, humble, mild, and erudite,
In the town of Olmutz in a priory he dwelled,
That old Brother Alfus, the monk the legends cite.

In lands all around in high esteem he was held,
His mind with vast knowledge did clearly overbrim,
For Science had graced him with gifts unparalleled.

Folks flocked from everywhere to catch a glimpse of him
Whose hair had gone white from the ferment in his brain,
But on one specific point his spirit was grim.

In reverie at dawn when great peace does obtain,
To the nooks of the garden he often betook,
Where the greenery sang from the fresh morning rain.

He listened to the breeze, to the birds and the brook,
But as his quest for answers led only to despair,
To his cell he returned, the garden he forsook.

You could see him stooped over like a tree in the square
For a tempest was brewing deep down in his soul
As Doubt like a stewing volcano rumbled there.

Into his simple faith the dagger of pride carved a hole
And his shoulders drooped from the internal pain —
Without a doubt Hell had come to collect its toll.

With prayer book in hand and finger to his brain,
He wandered past the willows and sometimes thought
That God may be a fiction and all our labors vain.

What purpose does it serve to dress in hairshirts taut,
Suppressing our desires until the day we die,
Living like the dead for a God that existeth not?

So festive they seemed, the birds and trees, the earth and sky,
But the monk's heart was flooded with voices malign,
And amidst the vast forest he began to cry.

## Notes

TITLE: At one hundred and nine lines, "Brother Alfus" is Nelligan's longest poem. It needn't be presented in its entirety; but since the poem is sometimes cited in Nelligan criticism, we can get a sense of it from the first of its three parts, comprising ten of the poem's total thirty-six tercets (three-line stanzas).

LINE 2: *Olmutz*. Now called Olomouc, this is a city in the historical region of Moravia, now in the modern Czech Republic. In late-medieval, pre-Reformation times, Moravia was subject to the Bohemian crown.

LINE 5: *overbrim*. This word, coming at the end of the second line of a three-line stanza, is required to rhyme with the first and third lines of the next three-line stanza. The verses are in *terza rima*, which follows the rhyme pattern ABA BCB CDC DED and so on. It's an energetic rhyme scheme that traces back to the beginnings of the Italian Renaissance when it was introduced by Alighieri Dante in his *Divine Comedy*.

## Comments

The legend of the holy monk Alfus, a medieval savant gnawed by religious doubts but saved by divine intervention, appeared from time to time in pious publications. It is possible Nelligan discovered the tale on his own. But it's tempting to believe that his friend Dantin, a priest riven by doubts, is the one who had Brother Alfus on his mind. Dantin has been suspected of secretly authoring the poem, not by writing it, no — an original in Émile's handwriting survives — but rather by planting it in Nelligan's head. It is a long narrative poem, the kind of thing Dantin himself liked to compose, but it bounces along at Nelligan's rhythms.

In the legend, the ratiocinating Alfus reaches the conclusion that Heaven, lacking the pleasures of Earth, must be an eternal bore. Therefore the afterlife is the same as no life at all. But Alfus's misgivings are overcome when God pulls him out of the temporal world to give him, in the blink of an eye, an overwhelming preview of Heaven's multi-sensory delights. God then places Alfus back on his path on Earth where he returns to his monastery only to learn that he has been absent for an entire century. Alfus thereupon praises God and dies on the spot.

.../

## Brother Alfus, Part I

Nelligan's version of the legend is a bit different. The monk, firmly planted in a Bohemian pastoral setting, is aggravated by the hairshirts and sensual deprivation that his holy vocation entails. If God does not exist, he reasons, if there is no heavenly reward, then all this self-repression makes him a fool. Thus Émile makes the monk's protest less cerebral and more a matter of sexual need, an issue that as a matter of fact was pertinent to both the juvenile Nelligan and the more experienced Dantin, priest of the Blessed Sacrament, who had left behind him in Belgium an unseemly liaison with a teenage girl.

Dantin had been a *Wunderkind* in Europe, studying in Paris and Rome where he achieved a doctorate in philosophy with honors. The Fathers of the Blessed Sacrament were so eager to enlist him that they initiated him at age 23, two years below their minimum-age rule. But already Dantin was arguing himself out of his faith; unlike Alfus, he never talked himself back into it. At the time when Nelligan met him, Dantin might very well wear a cassock but he had ceased his priestly functions such as celebrating Mass. He would quit the priesthood definitively in 1903, leaving Montreal with a lady friend, Clotilde Lacroix, and heading for Massachusetts. Disinherited by his family, Dantin continued to contribute to Quebec literature from a distance as a writer and critic, while plugging away at his day job as a typographer and proofer in Harvard University's printing house. He died in 1945 at age 80 and is buried in Boston.

Nelligan's "Brother Alfus" has the sort of pious ending that you'd think Dantin's *Petit Messager* magazine could have used: Alfus, after all his logic-making, is miraculously taken up into an immersive experience of Heaven where

> …ivory-white flowers wave in the breeze,
> The whole Eden quivers with ethereal chants
> And a hundred orbs echo their harmonies.

Nelligan's Alfus, like the original Alfus, returns to his monastery on Earth and dies on the spot. In a sense, this is another death poem. Heaven in its inimitable fashion has resolved all issues. Here is how "Brother Alfus" ends:

> As if offering up his soul, his arms he did raise,
> And he died cleansed of Doubt. His soul to heaven flew,
> That ancient monk Alfus, the one the legends praise.
> For us, by grace of God, may this also come true.

A curiosity about this uplifting finale is that, to take him at his word, the poet re-affirms the faith he was raised in. He is calm, resigned, he has at least for the moment come to terms with life and has imagined a rapturous view of the afterlife. He seems far from the troubled personality we might have feared to find, knowing of his eventual breakdown.

But Dantin did not publish this poem in his magazine, nor did he include it in his compilation *Émile Nelligan et son Œuvre*. Was there something about the poem that Dantin found uncomfortable? Was he too involved in its making? Did it remind him too much of himself?

~ ~ ~

## 23. Little Birds

Since Rusbrock instructs me —
Me, who feels naught but empathy
For all who seek to flee
    Misfortune's art —
To love you, I have brought
For you this dream I've got:
To make a landing spot
    Within my heart.

Here, wild birds in flight,
A shoreline you will sight,
A shelter from what plight
    The morrow brings:
Doves, swallows, hummingbirds,
Feathered friends, mark my words,
Your joy my dream engirds,
    Your bright flapping wings!

Dwell there safely everyone,
Of evening frost there shall be none,
For under the setting sun —
    That torch of gloom! —
Many a time in a bind
Assailed by gales unkind
Below the snow you find
    Your wintry tomb.

But shield you I forever will
From craven buckshot kill
And as stiffly I fulfill
    My sacrifice,
You, through the immense sky
Will guide me, by and by,
Knowing the way better than I,
    To Paradise.

## Notes

LINE 1: *Rusbrock*. Nelligan's spelling for John van Ruysbroeck, 14th-century Flemish mystic who wrote *The Seven Steps of the Ladder of Spiritual Love*. We need not surmise that Nelligan studied mysticism; he might have heard something of Ruysbroeck from Dantin.

## Comments

I count this as one of Nelligan's pious poems, leavened with what at first seems a touch of humor. The poem commences grandly with a mystic's message of love. The poet then resolves to give his love to wild birds by becoming a home for them. The under-current is that the poet is making a self-sacrificial bargain: he will become a landing place by dying and returning to the earth; the birds in exchange will guide his soul to heaven.

Nelligan is fond of birds. The aviary of his verse includes not just the doves, swallows and hummingbirds of this poem, but also, in other poems, an owl, an eagle, a vulture, a condor, and several crows and swans. Just one robin, though, which perishes in "Robin in the Woods" (poem 36).

~ ~ ~

## 24. Saint Cecilia

The lovely Saint high in the skies
Leads the orchestra angelical
In a distant hall basilical
Whose splendor dazzles my eyes.

Ever since the Virgin biblical
This holy calling did devise,
The lovely Saint high in the skies
Conducts the orchestra angelical

Far from this world diabolical,
I will hear amidst night-time sighs
Through all the realm where heaven lies,
Your harpsichord melancholical,

My lovely Saint high in the skies.

## Notes

TITLE: Saint Cecilia is the virginal patroness of musicians. This poem appeared in *La Patrie* in April 1899 under the title *L'Organiste des Anges*, the Organist of the Angels. Dantin renamed it *Sainte Cécile* in his 1904 compilation of Nelligan's work.

LINE 2: *angelical*. Rhymes ending in –ical in this translation reflect rhymes ending in –ique (*archangélique, basilique, biblique*, etc.) in the original. Nelligan learned the workability of this rhyme probably from reading French poet Maurice Rollinat, Nelligan's paragon for rhyme schemes.

LINE 5: *the Virgin biblical*. That is, the Virgin Mary also known as the Holy Mother and Queen of Heaven.

LINE 6: *This holy calling*. St. Cecilia is in charge of heavenly music.

## Comments

Nelligan had in mind to place this strongly musical rondel, evocative of medieval song, at the front of the book of verse he envisioned publishing in Paris one day. Sainte Cécile, accompanied typically by astral harps, is Émile's muse. Her figure rivals his mother's for the most attention in his poetry.

In days of the Roman Empire (so goes the myth), Cecilia, a Christian maiden of noble birth who had taken a vow of chastity, was given in marriage against her will. At the ceremony she sang out to the Lord in her heart, whereupon Heaven listened and sent an angel to convince her husband Valerian not to violate the vow. Thereupon, both Cecilia and Valerian went on to become shining Christians. Eventually, however, some sour imperial official made dead martyrs of them and when Cecilia rose up to her eternal reward, the Holy Mother placed her in charge of the music of Heaven.

.../

Saint Cecilia

Robertine Barry published this poem in *La Patrie*, fitting it without comment into her column, *Causerie Fantaisiste*, which roughly means Whimsical Words, on April 8, 1899. That was far from the saint's feast day, which is in November, but Robertine's column, with its exuberant mix of literature and popular journalism, was not fussy about topicality. Other items she included in her column that day informed readers about the invention of the ham omelette (by a medieval monk) and how to avoid conjugal jealousies (stop being so suspicious).

Robertine was at this time a phenomenon practically unheard of in Québec, not just a career woman but one earning her living in print. She hailed from the lower St. Lawrence shore where her dad was a lumber merchant. Her mother had borne thirteen children. Not coveting for herself the role of a wife, Robertine felt she had only two options: be a nun or be a writer. When Nelligan met her she was a columnist and section editor for the daily *La Patrie*. On Thursday afternoons she held salons for intelligent conversation in her home on rue Saint-Denis not far from Émile's home. He had only to walk three blocks north and three blocks east. Robertine advocated for free public libraries and for female higher education. To the end of her days she remained single, and defended singlehood as, so to speak, a vocation.

Nelligan was drawn to Robertine and would soon precipitate an amatory fiasco upon her. The denouement to that matter is discussed in the Comments to "Dark Virgin" (poem 39).

Émile had perhaps calculated that "Saint Cecilia" would specifically appeal to Robertine who was a Saint Cecilia devotee. There was a kind of Saint Cecilia cult in Québec, evidenced by a number of Saint Cecilia choral societies.

Religious poetry was a normal category in late 19th-century Québec. Nelligan wrote several pious poems that contrast with the poems of despair that later preoccupied him. One poem, *Petit vitrail* ("Little Stained Glass Window"), has Jesus smiling reassuringly at the poet from an ornate church window. Nelligan was absorbed in the *esthetics* of the Church, the light through stained glass, the music from the choir, the icons and flickering candles, the myths.

His outlook fluctuated. St. Cecilia, divine music-maker here in "Saint Cecilia", became silent and cold in "Immaculate Love" (poem 34). In the summer of 1899, only a few months after the publication of "Saint Cecilia", Nelligan was contemplating suicide and crumpling in the grip of Satan (see "Nocturnal Confession", poem 44), but perhaps that too should be considered religious poetry.

Readers of "Saint Cecilia" might wonder why Heaven's music would be melancholic. You have to pass through death to reach Heaven, of course. But more than that, melancholy was Nelligan's main disposition, it permeated his world and his creations; some people thought he turned it into a personal style. The sweetest music imaginable could not be other than melancholic.

A poem can be melancholy and remain pious as long as it respects the distinction between this sad world and the glories of the afterlife. "Saint Cecilia", like "Little Birds" (poem 23), arguably contains an implicit death wish — the poet longs to hear Heaven's melancholy harpsichord, which would presumably be the music of the instant of death.

~ ~ ~

## 25. The Bell in the Fog

Listen, listen, my wretched soul! That mournful knell
Away off in the fog — a bell! With somber might
Groaning in the gloom of the shivering night,
Touching our ears with the sorrow it has to tell.

What are you thinking? What is it you brood upon?
You who no longer pray — ah, could it be, poor thing,
That you measure your grief by the church bell's ring
That harks back to the angelus of days long gone?

Like that bell you mutter so monotone and drear,
Like that bell you jangle as autumn fogs grow near.
You're the plea of some church exiled to some dark space,

Absorbed in sonorous lament, seeking to cope
With the flight of the faithful from its holy embrace —
So very like yourself, an exile from all Hope.

## Notes

LINE 6: *You who no longer pray*. A fragment of Nelligan poetry survives entitled "The Death of Prayer".

LINE 8: *angelus*. In the heyday of worship, the angelus bell signaled the thrice-daily call to prayer — morning, noon, and evening.

## Comments

Émile tells us plainly that the empty church in the fog with the moaning bell equates to himself, a soul severed from Hope. That is how it is with Symbolists, they explain their symbols.

The poet is not the only disenchanted soul, for he says the faithful (in the plural) are quitting the church. This may reflect his bohemian milieu more than the population in general.

Nelligan often has bells sounding in his poems. A bell is a primal vibration, it speaks from ultimate reality, from Time itself. In Nelligan's work the bell is typically mournful, a leitmotif he may have picked up from Decadent poet Georges Rodenbach.

~ ~ ~

## 26. Christ on the Cross

A huge plaster Jesus every day I used to see,
A grim redeemer hung by the old abbey door,
And though the ambiance was bleak, I bowed before
That image, pious idolater that I be.

One evening, as crickets sang, through somber fields I passed,
Pondering how angels fall into fiery pits.
Distracted I was, hair tossing in the wind, as befits
A lad of artistic bent whose youth is fading fast.

Now beside the broken abbey walls I perceived
A large and heavy cross upon the rubble heaved,
While crumpled plaster over the primroses spread.

As I stood there, mournful, pondering what I'd found,
Inside me I felt a thousand hammers pound,
Driving deep the black nails in the Calvary of my head.

## Notes

LINE 4: *pious idolater*. Nelligan is aware, then, that Catholic icons invite idolatry.

LINE 6: *how angels fall into fiery pits*. In the French, the poet is roaming the fields while "reciting Éloa" which is to say reading aloud from the poem *Éloa* by Romantic poet Alfred de Vigny (1797-1863). The plot of *Éloa* is as follows: the angel Éloa, female in character, takes pity on the angel Lucifer who has rebelled against Heaven. She travels to his lair in hope of redeeming him. Lucifer, however, turns the tables by seducing Éloa, and since the latter sees no way back to Heaven, she accepts Lucifer as her lord.

LINE 7: *hair tossing in the wind*. Is the poet making fun of himself, striking this dramatic posture, a cliché of Romanticism? Nelligan does have a sense of humor from time to time. But this poem overall takes itself seriously.

LINE 8: *lad*. Nelligan says *éphèbe*, classical Greek word for a boy advancing into early manhood.

LINE 14: *black nails*. Black, because they convey a cosmic intensity of pain.

## Comments

Nelligan composed several poems that feature crumbling or abandoned church buildings. In truth, he has more ruined chapels than fits our image of a heavily churchgoing 19th-century Quebec society.

While ruins might be reliable scenic settings for Romanticism, the Symbolist in Nelligan would equate ruined chapels with collapsing faith.

The poet is in a field, in a gathering darkness, all meant to reinforce that the days of youth, the pastoral days, are a fading memory. The crumbled plaster Jesus on the rubble heap is the poet himself, on the trash heap of life.

~ ~ ~

## 27. October Roses

When autumn roses fall, you'll be spared that sight
If your dead heart inside my murdered heart be laid.
My grief, just like this month whose dazzling colors fade,
Plunges toward many an agonized night.

These crimson roses are an ugly blight,
Like sick red spots upon the woods displayed...
When autumn roses fall, you'll be spared that sight
If your dead heart inside my murdered heart be laid.

Look where the dreary cypress blocks the light —
One could get used to resting in its shade;
There, where a bed freshly dug waits ready-made,
Is where, my sweet, we two shall sleep tonight.

When autumn roses fall, you'll be spared that sight.

## Notes

LINE 2: *my murdered heart.* Nelligan says *mon cœur tué*, my heart that has been killed. Killed by what? A Decadent would say by industrial life, by materialism, by society, by the relentless march of time.

## Comments

There were several aspects of Nelligan's poetry that put it on the wrong side of the Church — his pro-suicide poems being a prime example. Here the poet explicitly enlists a lady friend in a death pact, which is surely a grave offense. It is as if he has resigned himself to being quite literally a *poète-maudit* in the sense of being a poet *damned.*

The poem is simultaneously a ferocious spoof of 16th-century Pierre de Ronsard's *Ode à Cassandre* wherein the poet persuades his companion that youth and beauty fade like roses therefore let us make love now. Nelligan arrives at a different conclusion: roses fade therefore let us put an end to the waiting now.

There's no avoiding Émile's abnormal obsession with death which can seem like a complete worldview: death is everywhere, because anything that has popped into existence is axiomatically on the way out.

"October Roses" arguably shows the influence of French-Belgian poet Georges Rodenbach whose themes of lost youth and *tempus fugit* resonated deeply with Nelligan starting from summer 1898.

~ ~ ~

## 28. Evening in Winter

Ah! How the snow did snow!
My window is a garden of frost.
Ah! How the snow did snow!
What a thing is the spasm of living
With all the pain that I know, that I know!

All the ponds lie frozen dead,
My soul is dark: Where am I? Where to go?
All my hopes lie frozen dead:
I am the new Norway
Whence the fair skies have fled.

Weep, birds of February,
At the evil vibration in things,
Weep, birds of February,
Weep for my roses, weep for my tears,
On the boughs of the juniper tree.

Ah! How the snow did snow!
My window is a garden of frost.
Ah! How the snow did snow!
What a thing is the spasm of living
With all the woe that I know, that I know!

## Notes

TITLE: Other translators have preferred to render the French title *Soir d'hiver* as "Winter Evening".

LINE 4: *spasm of living*. Nelligan is often linked to this phrase, *spasme de vivre*. He may himself have suffered from spasms.

LINE 9: *the new Norway*. That is, an *ultima Thule*, or northerly Land's End — from the European perspective that Nelligan absorbed in his readings.

## Comments

"Evening in Winter" is one of the most cited of Nelligan's poems. It is practically a sacred artifact in Quebec, rather like the song *Mon pays, c'est l'hiver* by Gilles Vigneault. Nelligan's poem was in fact made into a song by Claude Léveillée in 1965.

I expect that the poem belongs to February 1899, early in Nelligan's crisis year when he was weighed down with economic, romantic, and perhaps physical, pain.

I picture Nelligan looking out from inside his little room on the second floor at the front of the Nelligan home on avenue Laval. Through the frosted pane he sees birds on the bare branches of a juniper tree. Not far down the street is carré St.-Louis with its frozen pond. This evening in winter a downcast youth without practical prospects in the world sits at his window and composes a very competent sad song.

The final stanza repeats the first, bringing the poem back to where it started. The poet is enclosed in his room, frozen in place, the winter birds weep not just for him but for the evil vibration, the *sinistre frisson*, that runs through life.

~ ~ ~

## 29. A Poet

Let him be on his way, a dreamer passing by,
Let him live as he wants, no need to cause him strife.
His is an angelic soul, welcoming all of life,
Bearing within itself a glorious springtime sky.

His poetry is as pure as it is woebegone,
Like a golden whirlwind from inside him it swells.
A star understands it, that perfect star that dwells
In the glowing filigree of its celestial home.

He does not pry; he loves though no love come his way.
Let no one be concerned! Let no one spare a thought!
Say even that he's the dupe of his own plot!
Laugh at him! It matters not. We all must die some day.

And then beyond this world, where the Lord's kingdom lies,
With bitter reproach they'll show you the facts of the case,
What truth lay behind that proud and candid face,
What sorrow behind those grey and tearful eyes.

## Notes

LINE 1: *a dreamer passing by*. Nelligan was inspired by a poem in English by Arthur Guiterman (1871-1943) that begins, "He is a dreamer, let him pass". Nelligan's poem, like Guiterman's, is about a poet for whom a transcendent connection is part and parcel of his calling.

LINE 7: *A star understands it*. That is, a star as symbol of the shining ideal toward which the poet directs himself.

LINE 11: *the dupe of his own plot*. The poet lives with the thought that he may be proved a fool.

## Comments

Wyczynski (*Nell. Bio.*) says that "A Poet" is a reflection on the death of poet Georges Rodenbach who had come to the forefront of Nelligan's reading in late summer 1898. Rodenbach died from appendicitis at age 43 on Christmas Day of that year. The news would have been cabled across the Atlantic from France. This poem, then, belongs to the last days of 1898 or early 1899.

If you did not know that the poem is for Rodenbach, you might think Émile is complaining on his own behalf about the real or imagined ridicule a poet endures. He similarly complains about mockery in his famous "Wine Song" (poem 37).

Death enters the picture in blunt fashion in line 12. We *all must die some day* — spoken as if that consideration puts an end to all argument about the poet's folly or otherwise.

The poet in the end achieves a triumph based on the tenets of Catholic faith. In the afterlife, the good (the poet) will be honored while the wicked (those who mock the poet) will be rebuked.

Émile at least is still thinking that some form of heaven is available to him. The mental disaster of 1899 has not yet begun.

~ ~ ~

## 30. Rondel to My Pipe

I'll put my feet up to the fire,
And beer in hand, my finest pipe
(We're buddies of the broody type),
We'll share a dream, safe from winter's ire.

Against me heaven holds some gripe
And crowns my woes with flu so dire,
I'll put my feet up to the fire
And with our beer we'll dream, old pipe.

Death will come, the time is ripe,
This earthly hell must soon expire;
And when I'm sent to Satan's shire
I'll sit and smoke with that old type,

And put my feet up to the fire.

## Notes

TITLE: A rondel is a fixed form of thirteen lines using just two rhymes. When the lines are just eight syllables long, as here, you really feel the music. Nelligan addresses this poem to his faithful tobacco pipe.

## Comments

Nelligan offers what seems to be a humoristic and mildly irreverent interlude. "Rondel to My Pipe" starts with the poet at home sheltering from winter's blast, toasting his feet at the fireplace, medicating himself with beer and tobacco. Heaven, he complains, has added the flu to his list of woes on this Earth. He puffs his pipe and gazes into the flames. He's sick enough to die, and when he does, he expects that he'll be consigned to Hell. So be it! Smoking with that Satan fellow still beats winter up here!

Nelligan spins the tricks of comic effect. There's the *double entendre* of smoking. There's understatement, Satan is a *type*, a guy. There are twists such as how Heaven oppresses the poet but Hell welcomes him.

Émile does have a sense of humor that comes through now and then. He just didn't have enough of it to save himself. In later poems such as "Nocturnal Confession" (poem 44), Émile will not be so flippant about the prospect of damnation.

~ ~ ~

## 31. The Ghostly Ox

With ugly horns the great red ox
Across our peaceful fields does run,
Bellowing in the setting sun,
Horribly groaning as he stalks.

Everyone stops their friendly talks,
Their songs beneath the elm are done.
With ugly horns the great red ox
Across our peaceful fields does run.

Evil be its plans, beware everyone!
Cowboys in denim, girls in white frocks,
High to your neck pull up your socks!
Through fields and prickly bushes run,

Flee from the horns of the great red ox.

<u>Comments</u>

What is this rondel saying? First, what are the symbols? The field, the ox. Youth is trampled by some raging monster from the realm of the living dead. The ox does not have to be an external force. It could be internal. Nelligan ridicules and mourns pastoralism in several of his poems. Some anger, some obsession, some core issue drives him to upend the innocent pastoral world.

A rondel is a fixed-form poem restricted to two rhymes, while the first two lines of the first stanza form a refrain or chorus that returns at the end of the second stanza. The thirteenth and final line wraps the poem by echoing the first line. It sounds perhaps more complicated than it is. The outcome is guaranteed to be lyrical.

The rondel did allow certain variations. The 8-syllable lines (octosyllables) that Nelligan employs in "The Ghostly Ox" generate a lively, urgent poem. In several other rondels such as "Vase" (poem 41) Nelligan favors a 12-syllable (alexandrine) line which moves at a more pensive pace.

The rondel had its origins in medieval French love song, but it proved adaptable. Here Nelligan uses it to conjure a monstrous phantasm.

~ ~ ~

## 32. Hypochondriac Nights

The harpsichord begins to play
And then I grip my brow in fear
As dread compulsions have their way,

And as the faded chandelier
Casts sickly rays upon my face
Dark melodies command my ear.

From room to room half-crazed I race,
My eyes with tears filled to the brim,
I am forsaken in this place;

I'm cold as ice in every limb:
I want to kill myself but how?
December, how your nights are grim!

O cursed angels, help me now!

## Notes

LINE 13: *cursed angels*. Nelligan says *anges maudits*, which would be Lucifer and his cohorts that were banished from Heaven.

## Comments

Suicide, a recurring theme in Nelligan, had a mystique in the 19th-century Romantic tradition: the artist who chose suicide demonstrated a certain ascendance over society.

One of Nelligan's idols, Baudelaire, at age 23, announced his intention to kill himself and actually did stab himself before his girlfriend Jeanne Duval came to the rescue.

One factor that makes "Hypochondriac Nights" exciting is the interlocking *terza rima* rhyme scheme: ABA BCB CDC DED and so on. Here's how Edward Hirsch (*A Poet's Glossary*) explains *terza rima*:

> Rhyming the first and third lines gives each tercet a sense of temporary closure; rhyming the second line with the first and last lines of the next stanza generates a feeling of propulsion. It is like moving through a series of interpenetrating rooms or going down a set of winding stairs: you are always traveling forward while looking back.

Nelligan composed this poem in a dark phase over the winter of 1898-99. Despite the title, readers may feel the poet's condition is more correctly high anxiety rather than hypochondria. Nelligan, however, wanted to allude to the poem *L'Hypocondriaque* by French Decadent poet Maurice Rollinat, wherein the poet finds nothing at the bottom of his soul but the thought of death, presumably the ultimate in hypochondria. Compared to Rollinat, Nelligan's poem is quicker, more tormented, more frightening: Nelligan summons Lucifer and actively *plunges* toward death.

~ ~ ~

# 33. Our Lady of the Snows

Our Holy Lady, in cloak golden bright
    From her land so flowery
Descends, while Jesus is resting at night,
    Unto her Ville-Marie.
By starry torches the angels hold high,
    The lovely Virgin comes
Triumphantly, as melodies fill the sky,
    And the lute of heaven thrums.

On her throne up high our Holy Lady dwells,
    On our Mount Royal it sits;
The Satyr with just one glance she repels
    To his infernal pits.
For she has said, "May an angel protect
    With an arm of fire true
My city of silver in snow bedecked,"
    The Lady of sky-blue!

O quick, Holy Lady, rescue this land
    Where only you shall reign;
Oust the outsider! Be the saving hand
    For our wintry domain.
This petition that with golden words we write,
    May you with your own eyes
Peruse it in the rosy evening light
    When you descend from the skies!

Long has our Holy Lady shed her tears
    With her angels gathered round;
So much, they say, that all of heaven hears
    The ringing mystical sound,
And they say that our Virgin will restore —
    How glorious this will be! —
A Garden of Eden where bloom once more
    Her France and her Ville-Marie...

## Notes

TITLE: In Catholic legend, in Rome in August of the year 352, the Holy Mother miraculously caused a patch of snow to appear on the spot where she wanted a church built. In Montreal her name is taken up by Cimetière Notre-Dame-des-Neiges, a cemetery on the north flank of Mount Royal.

LINE 4: *Ville-Marie*. That is, Montréal, established in the 17th century as a mission station named Ville-Marie, which means Mary's Town. Our Lady, also known as the Blessed Virgin Mary, is thus Montréal's divine protector.

LINE 10: *Mount Royal*. That is, Mont Réal, the sacred mountain around which the city of Montréal grew. The city's founder Paul de Chomedey de Maisonneuve climbed to the summit to plant a legendary oaken cross in pioneer days.

LINE 11: *Satyr*. Nelligan says *le Faune* which derives from the Roman *Faunus*, a goat-man divinity like Pan, but with emphasis on carnality.

LINE 19: *Oust the outsider!* The French is *Chasse l'etranger!* That is, chase away the outsider, conceivably referring back to the devil of line 11, but, given the religio-cultural thrust of this poem, even more conceivably referring to the Anglo-Scottish business class that had ruled Montreal's economy since the Conquest of 1760.

LINE 32: *Her France and her Ville-Marie*. France and Montreal. Such a fantasy merger would amount to Nelligan's poetic heartland.

## Comments

Nelligan presented this poem at a public session of the École Littéraire in February 1899. As elsewhere in Nelligan's poetry, the oedipal overtones are striking. This time it's the Holy Mother in her golden cape protecting a white-lace city against an intrusive satyr.

*...*/

Our Lady of the Snows

Yet the poem is about something else too. It's as close as Nelligan comes to a Quebec nationalist statement. Keep in mind that 19th-century Quebec nationalism had a strong religious component. Religious symbols were nationalistic in the sense that they were ingrained in Quebec culture, they provided a connection with the pre-Conquest past. The poem claims to speak on behalf of *nous* — that is, on behalf of the Catholic francophone audience. Holy Mother, the poet says, come rescue this land!

At this time the Dominion of Canada, as such, was barely a generation old, Confederation in 1867 being merely the latest in a number of shaky political arrangements for British North America. Émile's dad worked for the dominion government as a postal inspector.

Would French survive? That wasn't clear. In Montréal, the key metropolis, Anglophone economic dominance and share of the population were growing. In rural areas there was a drain of population looking for better economic prospects in the northeastern United States.

It appears, then, that a few tendrils of Émile's consciousness had touched upon Quebec nationalism. We know that along with a few fellow poets he joined the large crowd on November 1, 1896, attending a ceremony at the monument to Honoré Mercier, a political figure who had opposed Confederation and who led the opposition to the execution of Métis resistor Louis Riel.

Nelligan was the tenth of eleven speakers the night he recited "Our Lady of the Snows" at the École Littéraire, which was not a school in the sense of providing instruction or espousing a particular literary doctrine. The École's purpose was to stimulate a francophone literary scene, surely an inherently nationalistic endeavor. Nelligan was the son of an Irish immigrant, but he opted for North American French culture.

The embrace of France conjured by Nelligan in line 32 of this poem might not have seemed fanciful, given a colonial way of thinking wherein the colony reflexively looks to the homeland for support. Just as English-Canadian literati in the late 19th century looked to London for literary leadership, francophones looked to Paris. The honorary president of the École Littéraire was Louis Fréchette, the Québec *poète national* of his day; his prestige partly derived from a literary prize that had been awarded him in 1880 by the Académie Française. He could boast that on his Paris trip he had conversed with the illustrious Victor Hugo, the very epitome of French literature! Such small steps helped Quebeckers gather faith in their own literary culture which would eventually thrive.

A further feature of this poem is that it is a rare instance of Nelligan actually identifying in his verses his home city of Montréal. Generally the sole indications of *terroir* expressed in his work are references to the seasons of the year. Winter, spring and autumn are especially appreciated for their symbolic value. In this poem, Nelligan incorporates winter in faintly inconsistent ways. The season of snow is a sparkling décor for the Holy Lady and her adopted city, but it is also implicitly a moribund condition to be overcome in the closing lines by a season of bloom.

Incidentally, after his death in 1941 Nelligan was interred on the flank of Mount Royal in Cimetière Notre-Dame-des-Neiges, that is, the Our-Lady-of-the-Snows Cemetery. His mother and father are buried there, and his sister Gertrude likewise.

~ ~ ~

## 34. Immaculate Love

A wondrous stained glass adorns a church I know
Where some acclaimed artist, by archangels inspired,
Has painted in mystic mode, in flowing robes attired,
A blue-eyed Saint, face haloed by an astral glow.

In the night, my mind tormented by murky dreams
And the otherworldly echo of an eerie choir,
I go to pray to her, in rays as orange as fire
From the light of the moon that through her blond hair gleams.

That's how upon the stained glass of my heart I did paint
My novelesque beloved, my blond and pale Saint —
That's you, the only one I love and always will.

But you stay silent, self-contained and prideful still,
Amused to observe me, wretched and ill-starred,
Wandering in my love as in a cold graveyard.

## Notes

LINE 1: *a church I know*. In Notre Dame Basilica in Montreal there is a stained glass representation of St. Cecilia that comes close to matching the description Émile gives here, although that is not necessarily to say that he is staging this poem in that building.

LINE 5: *night*. It is late enough that in line 8 the moon is beaming strongly.

LINE 10: *My novelesque beloved*. The poet says, *Ma romanesque aimée*, suggesting that he considered his beloved to be the kind of exceptional character one might encounter in a novel, *un roman*. In French, *un personnage romanesque* is a character in a novel. Nelligan is in addition punning on another use of *romanesque* as a type of church architecture.

## Comments

In a pattern typical of Nelligan the mood of the poem develops from ethereality to dejection. First we have the beauteous Cecilia, blond saint of music. The poet prays to her in the moonlight. Then he explains: this blond saint that I paint is the picture of you that's graven on my heart. I'm floundering, he complains, and it merely amuses you.

What was his blond saint being cold and silent about? What had the poet expected of her?

"That's you", the poet says. You who? Whoever the subject of this poem was, the poem reads as though meant to be directly handed to her. We know, for instance, that Émile handed a poem titled "To a Detested Woman" to Robertine Barry who likewise had turned him down.

In a Roman Catholic society, the word "immaculate" resonates as "spotless" in the sense of "sin-free". The use of the word in the title for this poem looks like irony — the idea being that the affair was not consummated, therefore the love was immaculate.

~ ~ ~

## 35. The Black Girl's Tomb

Once the winds of winter released us from their blast,
We carried her, in March, under an ashen sky,
Into a gloomy cinnamon-scented grove nearby
Where hints of fresh verdure poked through the soil at last.

On branches overhead various birds amassed,
Each one in its innocent heart heaving a sigh.
In the rough humid earth where this African will lie,
May she slumber in peace as the green months slip past.

Piously the earth will hold her coffin tight
While the red finch above from a perch in his tree
Will sing his lament how her twenty years were so slight.

Returning in some distant spring, perhaps we'll see
Among the shrubs, that from her heart has come to be
A great black lily blooming amidst the roses white.

## Notes

LINE 7: *African*. Poetic license. Or an outdated figure of speech. There's no need to suppose the young woman actually was from Africa, black people at this time having lived in Canada for many generations.

LINE 11: *her twenty years*. The number twenty was significant for Nelligan, who had a sense that youth ends at age twenty. He told us so in one of his poems, *La fuite de l'Enfance* (not included in this collection), where he speaks of "the flight of Youth on the ship of Twenty Years".

## Comments

There was a late 19th-century fad for *poèmes-tombeaux,* tomb poems, monuments erected on paper in homage to departed poets. Stéphane Mallarmé had erected tomb poems for Edgar Allan Poe and Charles Baudelaire, for example. The idea was bound to appeal to death-obsessed Nelligan, who went on to write tomb poems for Chopin and, again, Baudelaire.

In "The Black Girl's Tomb", Nelligan is honoring not one of his artistic idols but rather an ordinary person, or someone who would be ordinary were she not distinguished by her skin color, which was shared by a small minority of Montrealers at that time. Nelligan for whatever reason had an interest in black persons, who appear in several of his poems. He may have felt like a minority himself.

*Noir*, black, in some cases translated as "dark," is the most frequent color-word in Nelligan's verse, and often it is freighted with negative symbolism as the color of evil or the void. But here the poet is talking about *real* black, the color of flesh. At the end comes the twist as he returns to a symbolic way of thinking, painting a shining picture of a black lily blooming amidst white roses. Émile turns black into a symbol of hope and indomitability, a promise even of transformation, of afterlife.

~ ~ ~

## 36. Robin in the Woods

As we sat reading Werther beneath a forest tree,
Upon a bough above us a robin did alight,
And as he sang his tune I clasped your hands so white
And spoke the words of love you've often heard from me.

But you were heedless of my true and simple plea,
Mute to my confession of the feelings you excite;
All at once, off you ran amongst the flowers bright,
Until, shaken, you called my name and cried "Come see!"

What tumbled from the trembling leaves was in the end
The sentimental robin, the springtime's poor friend
Who in that instant died, struck down in his prime.

And you, you wept for him, for his song now gone by,
While me, I thought as I gazed at the vast blue sky:
Love and the Robin died at the very same time.

## Notes

LINE 1: *Werther*. Refers to Goethe's 1774 novel *The Sorrows of Young Werther*. The protagonist, Werther, is a passionate young artist who, stung by disappointment in love, kills himself. A Werther-inspired wave of copycat suicides in 19th-century Europe is remembered in history as the "Werther fever".

## Comments

Here Nelligan combines one obsessional theme, death, with another obsessional theme, the failure of love. It's springtime but the poet wants to talk about a doom-laden book. Does he hope his companion will take pity on him? But no, she rushes away, off into bright nature, only to bump smack into death in the form of a dead robin. Nelligan capitalizes "Robin" in the last line. A songbird is a symbol for a poet, and this poet has been mortally wounded. The poem commemorates the end of a courtship.

~ ~ ~

# 37. Wine Song

In springtime's festive joy all the world combines:
The birds in choir sing, this fine evening in May,
Much like the hopes that filled my heart just yesterday,
Trilling at my window their prelude to these lines.

A fine evening in May, a joyful eve in May!
A distant organ hums its cold and steady chords;
The sun's descending rays impale like crimson swords
The heart of day, which sweetly perfumed dies away.

So happy am I! Into this singing crystal ware
Pour, pour the wine, for ever and ever pour!
Until I remember these wretched days no more,
And what the vile crowd says, I never shall care.

I'm happy, so happy. A toast to wine and to art!
I too have dreams of writing verse adored by all,
Verses that wail like the mournful winds in fall
That you hear passing in fog in a land far apart.

A life of rage and bitter laughter is my right
For being a poet that all the world does shun,
For being a soul that is understood by none
Except by the moon and the great stormy night.

Ladies, I drink to you who mock the path I take
Where a vision holds me in its sultry embrace;
Here's to you, most of all, you men of sullen face,
Who scorn my life and snub the hand I give to shake.

While stars in their glory bejewel the night-time sky
Rehearsing their hymn to greet the golden dawn,
I, in my darkened youth, groping blindly on,
Shed not a single tear to see the daytime die.

I'm so happy, so happy, and I'm sloshed not a bit;
I'm insanely happy — to evenings in May I drink!
It could be that at last I'm glad to live, I think:
Having once loved, has my heart finally healed from it?

The bells have chimed; the breeze brings twilight's fragrant shroud,
And as long as some joyous stream of wine appears
Then I am happy, happy, laughing right out loud,
Oh so happy that I fear I shall burst into tears!

## Notes

TITLE: The title in French is *La romance du vin*, the word *romance* meaning a sentimental song, most often a love song.

LINE 4: *at my window*. Nelligan says *à ma croisée ouverte*, at my open crossbar window. The word *croisée* suggests the lattice of mullions and crossbars that make up a multi-paned window. A symbolist might see a field of crucifixes therein.

LINE 9: *So happy am I*. Nelligan says *je suis gai*, which would be reckless nowadays to translate as "I am gay". The word *gai* in late 19th-century French primarily meant, like English *gay* at that time, merry, light-hearted, and in some contexts, tipsy.

LINE 33: *The bells have chimed*. The vespers bells for evening prayer.

## Comments

Nelligan's recital of "Wine Song" on May 26, 1899 at a public session of the École Littéraire de Montreal at Château de Ramezay in Old Montreal, that is, at the core of the sacred memory of the old French regime, is treated by Nelligan biographers as a momentous event. The hall was packed, which at the start of the evening meant about 300 attendees, all avid to encourage French Canadian culture amidst irreversibly and overwhelmingly anglophone North America.

Émile was one of the youngest members of the École. He had passed an audition to join the club shortly after quitting regular school in early 1897. This was a reasonable career move. He could air his work at the École and get critiqued. Almost two years later, by reciting at the club's public sessions, Émile was declaring himself a public poet.

Had he not so anxiously sought fame, he might not have been so stung by the criticism he received. Nelligan grew depressed after reading a dismissive review of his work in *Le Monde illustré* in March of 1899 penned by Édouard de Marchy. Nelligan's verse had not appeared in that publication

.../

## Wine Song

for almost a year, which might indicate a falling-out. At the end of his review, with the stated purpose of encouraging young poets, de Marchy invited Nelligan to debate poetry with him in the journal's pages.

Nelligan was downcast, but his friends including Dantin and Robertine, convinced him to continue to participate in the club's readings. On this famous May 26, then, Nelligan would recite three poems, of which "Wine Song" would be the middle one.

Dantin and others have touted "Wine Song" as Émile's "response" to de Marchy, they have called it Émile's artistic "manifesto", as if he were like the poets of Paris, habitually issuing manifestos about poetic revolutions. It's true that "Wine Song" is forceful, it bristles with exclamation marks, but it is dipsomaniac and it hardly amounts to a credo. The poet asserts a right to be what he is; beyond that, the poem is more of a plaint.

The initial images are of nature abloom in spring, instantly reminding the poet that he too once held hopes of blossoming. For him, a festive world conjures personal grief.

Hence, wine. The poet calls for wine. Drink and be happy! These words no doubt helped to nourish the idea that Nelligan was an unrestrained drinker. Maja Nazaruk in the *Montreal Review* of April 2013 felt that Nelligan on this occasion was setting himself up as a Dionysian priest. Certainly Nelligan the Symbolist would have in mind that wine, manifesting the fiery essence of life, is a sacrament.

Next, bitterness. The poet wants to forget. He dreams of writing famous verse, he says, and he gives samples of how lyrical he can be. But, alas, it is his fate to be a poet-outsider understood by no one, "except by the moonlight and the great stormy night".

Is de Marchy really the target of Nelligan's verses? The poet more palpably expresses resentment against certain categories of people: the women who mock him for being a hapless poet, and the men who treat him with disdain. Such people might be in the very audience he is addressing. No matter! The poet sees an upside, which is that he is so plastered that he can finally believe that he is cured of love.

So at the bottom of this drunken manifesto lies the tale of a broken heart. I'm so happy, the poet says, I'm so happy, I'll burst into tears.

A story was later constructed that portrayed Nelligan's recital of this poem on May 26 as an immense triumph. The audience supposedly went delirious, they tossed their hats in the air, they carried the poet home on their shoulders. That was a picture that long stood in Quebec literary myth. But if there was such a "triumph", it didn't make the papers. *La Patrie* in its review the next day merely listed Nelligan's name among several speakers it said it lacked space to discuss. *La Presse* allotted Nelligan a dozen not unkind words — the poet is a dreamer whose verses evoke sweet music, the paper said — but gave no hint that Nelligan had brought the house to a roar. At *Le Monde illustré*, meanwhile, de Marchy was as dismissive as ever, ranking Émile sixth-best of the seven poets who stood at the podium that evening. Month after month, de Marchy consistently ranked Nelligan last or near-last in his reviews.

"Wine Song" nevertheless is a poem of merit. It's straight from the heart. Nelligan's junior status meant that he was typically slotted to recite his verses at the tail-end of the club's line-up when the crowd might have thinned out. But anytime you are crying *Vive le vin!* and *Vive l'art!* you are liable to provoke a boisterous response from the die-hards and devotees that remain.

There may have been enough cheers to be exaggerated into a "triumph" by Dantin and by members of the École in later years as they discovered themselves annexed to Nelligan's history.

One way or the other, Émile never reaped the benefit of any triumph. He never returned to the École. He felt that the old guard was hostile to his poetry and that the young poets were maneuvering against him. From that moment, the picture is that a downtrodden Nelligan sequesters himself in his room writing feverish verses. By the second week of August he is in an asylum.

That is the Nelligan legend that long resonated in Quebec, the story of the sparkling triumph of the home-grown poet, followed oddly, cruelly, in tragic 19th-century Romantic fashion, by madness.

~ ~ ~

## 38. The Haunted Pit

In the dark pit that you see there
Lies the source of this sad tale.
Within the woods the stag's loud wail
Relates the gist of this affair.

There was a mad lover, that's where
The fool was drowned by some female.
In the dark pit that you see there
Lies the source of this sad tale.

Psst! That eerie glow — beware!
At night a soul is burning pale:
You hear it moaning raspy and frail
As in some ghostly country fair

In the dark pit that you see there.

## Notes

LINE 5: *mad lover*. Louis Dantin's edition of 1904 has *amant fou*, mad lover, which is the version I use here. Dantin in later years claimed that the original phrase had been *prêtre fou* (mad priest), which he had been obliged to change to guard against Catholic sensitivities. The original manuscript that Dantin was working with is lost, however. I prefer the *amant fou* reading since it seems to me more likely that Nelligan would be generalizing from his own passion rather than that of an unnamed priest.

## Comments

A burning soul, drowned by some *femme fatale*. This brisk rondel is influenced in tone and style by the example of Maurice Rollinat, one of the so-called Decadents, a poetic current that emerged in late 19th-century France. The Decadents were the Fancy Dans of the macabre. Nelligan gravitated to them in late 1898. In virtuosity and vitality, as this poem shows, Nelligan's rondels could match or outdo the masters.

A rondel can have only two rhymes, and the first two lines of the first stanza must be repeated as the last two lines of the second stanza. Then the poem's first line is repeated again as its last line. The final product is intensely circular, self-enclosed, obsessional with no way out. Closed loops are one of the most striking features of Nelligan's verses. For another example, see "October Roses" (poem 27).

~ ~ ~

## 39. The Dark Virgin

Like exotic torches in her eyes a fire glows.
Strands of false-gold hair across thin shoulders spray,
Like skittering foliage in willowy array:
She's like a cypress that amongst the gravestones grows.

Sullen and wicked, in raggedy garb she goes,
But whether in some prison you lock her away,
Or with steel-tipped whips you beat her day after day
— Beware, mortal men, hers is the color of crows.

She smiled on me once from the vast depth of her soul,
I thought her my friend and insouciant we would stroll,
Always sticking together, we two, hand in hand.

But when, dark with desire, to her one day I came,
She told me, "Your foul footsteps have sullied my land".
You surely must know this woman: Life is her name.

## Notes

TITLE: The French title is *La vierge noire;* the word *noire* covers a color range from black to dark. When Nelligan speaks of *anges noirs,* for example, in English we would usually say "dark angels". Here Nelligan is talking less about the color than about connotations of obscurity and evil.

LINE 8: *the color of crows.* That is, an ill omen.

## Comments

This is another of Nelligan's 'dark' poems — they add up to a fairly long list. Dark ponds, dark bells, even dark toys (darkened by sad memory) pervade his work. In one poem, *Musiques funèbres,* Nelligan speaks of life's "dark carillon" accompanying us to the end.

Pierre Lemieux (*Nell. Am.*) contends that "The Dark Virgin" is a summary of Nelligan's "misadventure" with Robertine Barry, 16 years older than himself. Judging by these verses, Émile went to her "dark with desire", but the idea of accommodating the young man's desire plainly repulsed her. She would rather be a virgin.

How solid a prospect is Émile, frankly? He's a nervous type, melancholy, and his career plan is to make a living from poetry, something unheard of in Canada then and even now.

"The Dark Virgin" joins a passel of missives aimed at poor Robertine. Others were "To a Detested Woman" and "Cruel Beauty" (not included in this collection), titles that tell you almost all you need to know. The young man was bitter and wounded to the core, even if objectively the match-up was implausible.

It's a misogynist poem, Lemieux says. It's difficult to argue against that, unless maybe love/hate partakes of a different order. The twist at the end of "To a Detested Woman" is that the poet asks himself why he is crying.

Nelligan actually maximizes his plaint, reaching beyond Robertine: the dark virgin that rejects him is "Life".

~ ~ ~

## 40. Castles in Spain

I dream of striding bold like a conquistador,
A valiant holy warrior full of fiery pride,
My labarum held high, a legend far and wide,
Against golden-towered cities waging war.

Like regal bird, like eagle, vulture or condor,
High in the heavenly sphere I want to glide,
My wings bursting aflame as past the sun I slide
In my quest to seize the celestial Treasure store.

But I am no mounted knight nor giant bird of prey;
For scarcely can I mount sufficient self-control
To overcome the age-old Demons in my soul.

My high-flying dreams like candles melt away
Before eternal Troy, city of a hundred walls,
Love's vestal Virgin citadel that never falls!

## Notes

TITLE: The phrase "castles in Spain" has the same connotation in French as in English, namely, that of unrealizable projects, chimera.

LINE 3: *labarum*. This was the Roman military standard topped by the monogram *chi-rho*, being the first two letters of the name Christ (*Khristos*) in Greek. The labarum is commemorated in Catholic lore since it was carried by Constantine the Great who seized the imperial throne and made Christianity the official religion of the Roman Empire. "Under this sign you shall conquer," God purportedly proclaimed to Constantine at the illustrious Battle of Milvian Bridge in the year 312 CE.

LINE 7: *My wings bursting aflame*. Alluding to the myth of Icarus who flew too close to the sun.

LINE 8: *Treasure*. Nelligan often capitalizes key words, to intensify their allegorical power. The quest to seize Heaven's Treasure suggests the myth of Prometheus, who filched fire from the gods.

LINE 11: *age-old Demons*. Nelligan says *les vieux Anges impurs*. In Catholic demonology, these are fallen angels who, having become agents of Satan, take control of your mind and body, even of your voice.

LINE 13: *eternal Troy*. The Troy of the *Iliad* may have fallen, but the eternal Troy in the realm of the Ideal can never be breached, encircled as it is, the poet says, by a hundred walls. Conquest therefore was impossible from the beginning.

## Comments

This sonnet, brimming with both Christian and classical mythological allusions, is a story of impossible love. Emile Talbot (*Reading Nell.*) particularly aided my understanding of this poem.

It's an alexandrine sonnet, which is to say it consists of fourteen 12-syllable lines divided into four stanzas in a contrapuntal structure that Nelligan seemed to like: the two quatrains (the four-line stanzas) elaborate a situation or argument that is subsequently challenged by the two tercets (the three-liners).

.../

Castles in Spain

In the first quatrain, the poet declares his dream-wish: he wants to be a conquistador, winning renown by conquering a fortified city. In the second quatrain, he wants to fly so high that his wings will burst into flames. This wish, at mid-poem, forewarns of disaster. The poet is calling to mind the Icarus of Greek myth who flew too close to the sun and plummeted back to earth, a blazing failure.

Why is the poet willing to risk so much high-altitude damage? It's all for the glory of executing a Promethean raid on a forbidden capital-T Treasure.

While the Christian myth that launches this poem is associated with victory, the pagan mythology that soon follows is closer to the reality the poet feels. In line 7 there's that clear allusion to Icarus who, notably ignoring his father's warnings, flies so impermissibly high that a furious Sun incinerates his feeble wings of feather and wax and sends him tumbling to the sea.

In line 8 the poet alludes to Prometheus, another striver, who steals fire from the gods. His remuneration for this inestimable boon to mankind is that he is chained to a rock and Zeus sends an eagle to peck at his liver. Hence in two lines we have two cases of someone being persecuted for demanding more than the gods allow.

The theme of a fall from heights is frequent in Nelligan's verses. A repeated feature is the reversal from expectant opening to negative closure. It may seem to us that someone so young as Nelligan should not be so ready to concede. It's true that he has had romantic disappointments, most recently Robertine Barry. Proposing to her, a successful journalist sixteen years older than himself and committed to singlehood — now, that was the impossible project that might explain line 14.

Added to that setback was the bleak prospect for profit in his poetical career. And why shouldn't it be called a career, since it consumed all of his time? That pointed to a third area of failure, the deterioration of life at home. For Nelligan, all of this was an oppressive load to bear.

Returning now to consider the structure of the poem, the first line of the first tercet is known as the *volta*, an Italian term indicating a turning point: the *volta* spins the poem in a different direction from the one it seemed to set out for. "I am no mounted knight nor giant bird of prey," the poet concedes. Why, he can't defeat his own demons, let alone conquer a mighty city.

The final tercet deepens the mortification by demonstrating that the poet's entire quest was founded on illusion. His dreams melt like candles — the perfect image to remind us of Icarus's melting wings. The poem that started with bravado ends in misery. Now we see clearly what that fortified city was, what that Treasure was — it was the impenetrable citadel of Love.

~ ~ ~

## 41. Vase

It's an Egyptian vase shaped with exquisite care,
Whereon blue-painted sphinxes and amber lions lie,
And that lithe, softly curving silhouette nearby
Is immutable Isis teasing out her hair.

Bright golden ships glide by, no sails do they bear,
Across silver waters beneath a marbled sky;
It's an Egyptian vase shaped with exquisite care,
Whereon blue-painted sphinxes and amber lions lie.

My soul is a vase, a faded ill-shapen ware
That holds the tears my hopes have shed in times gone by;
I suffer deep inside where raging fires flare,
But all will be smashed soon enough when I die…

For my life is a vase that was shaped without care.

## Notes

LINE 4: *Isis*. Egyptian mother-goddess and Queen of Heaven.

LINE 10: *holds the tears*. Referring to the practice of saving tears in a tear bottle.

LINE 13: *shaped without care*. According to a common model of the rondel, the last line echoes the first line, perhaps with a clever twist. Nelligan's last line *repudiates* the initial premise. The poem travels from perfection to deformity, from paradise to abandonment.

## Comments

This is one of Nelligan's 'furniture' poems, the kind of thing symbolists liked to assemble. The idea was to make a metaphor of this or that *objet*. An old piano, for example, might be a washed-up poet, as it is in Nelligan's poem *Vieux piano*. A vase likewise has symbolistic possibilities. It is uterine. It could hold treasure. But what seems most important in this case is that it is a surface for a beautiful timeless world.

The poem shows how truly Parnassian Nelligan could be before veering into self-pity. Note the calm iteration of the stately images, serene Isis eternally tending her hair, the golden ships gliding motionlessly over a notional Nile. The whole idea of ancient Egypt is of a static world. Look again at Isis, irresistible yet unattainable, sensual in principle but frozen in time.

Émile sweeps serenity off the page in the last few lines. Now his soul is a deformed vase, his hopes have melted into tears, and he looks forward to death.

What hopes melted into tears? Hopes of love, one can guess. The poet plainly feels unloved. And since the de Marchy crisis, it may be that Émile is losing faith in the dream of publishing in Paris; with that gone there will be nothing left.

~ ~ ~

## 42. I Want to Lose Myself

I want to lose myself in laughter,
Of the gruff merry mob I'll be part,
Yes, self-delusion will be my art,
With hysterical fits coming after.

What monstrous vampires — O pity, please! —
Come sucking blood from my wounded heart!
Oh I want to go mad, if only to depart
With a show of disdain for my Agonies.

Slow like a beast from the living dead,
The ship of my heart will always head
To the harbor of some motley crowd.

How I thank those masters of disrespect
With their railleries so crude and loud
That mock the innocent Intellect.

### Notes

LINE 5: *monstrous vampires*. The folklore legend of vampires had acquired new life in 19th-century literature, crowned by Bram Stoker's novel *Dracula* in 1897.

LINE 10: *The ship of my heart*. Nelligan often employs the boat image. The ship of his heart will sink forever in one of his best-known creations, "The Ship of Gold" (poem 45).

### Comments

This sonnet is often cited as an example of Nelligan willing madness upon himself, based mainly upon line 7 where he specifically says he wants to go mad. This poem is presumed to have been composed between June and August of 1899, in the crescendo of his nervous crisis. After Émile's breakdown, the poem survived as a scrap that was not edited and made public until 1952.

Nelligan had declared to his friends that he would probably go mad. Dantin thought this was part of Émile's *poète-maudit* posturing. There had been a kind of consecration of madness among the literati of late 19th-century Europe. Madness proved you had spirit. There was supposedly a link between madness and genius.

Nelligan self-identified as a neurotic poet in an inhospitable world. He might very well have wished to escape that world. Still, would someone choose madness as a destiny? Maybe for Émile it was too late, maybe he had gone so far that there was no way back. To wilfully choose madness, would you not have to be mad in the first place?

~ ~ ~

## 43. The Crows

I swear upon my heart I saw a flock of crows
That passed in mournful flight across my inner slue,
Enormous crows that down from fabled mountains flew
By the light of the moon and flaming flambeaus.

As if circling a tomb, ever closer they did close,
As if sensing some zebra carcass to chew,
On my spine they settled, cold spasms ripped through,
As they tore open my flesh with pitiless blows.

Now, this prey that fell before the demons of the nights
Is nothing but my tattered Life with all its plights
That circle around it in ravenous ways:

Into raggedy strips their beaks slice my soul,
As though it were carrion spread on the field of days
That these old crows have arrived to devour whole.

### Notes

LINE 9: *demons of the nights*. Nelligan uses the plurals. In the summer of 1899 Émile endured multiple mental torments, including nightmares, succubae, and insomnia.

### Comments

Black is the most oft-named color in Nelligan's poetry, but you need not name a color to conjure it. Here Nelligan paints a black on black dreamscape of crows flying across the night sky, with moonlight and torches providing fiery accents.

This sonnet belongs probably to the winter of 1898-99, a time when Émile was turning to the macabre verses of American Edgar Allan Poe (1809-1849). Nelligan, a keen reader of English-language poetry as well as French, knew Poe's "The Raven" by heart and tentatively worked on a French translation of the poem. But Nelligan's crows, unlike Poe's, are more than just omens, they are demonically aggressive.

The intensity of pain related by the poet, not just in this poem but in others as well — "Christ on the Cross" (poem 26), for example — supports speculation that Nelligan's condition included neurological pain.

~ ~ ~

## 44. Nocturnal Confession

Padre, it's night in town, by demons I'm possessed,
Mortal sins have turned my soul into a torture room,
Upon the boulevards there pours a torrent of gloom,
And no one from the lowly plebs attends this fest.

All quiet, all asleep. This lonely Town so depressed
Sickens from this horror show where hoary houses loom;
Padre, it's night in town, by demons I'm possessed,
Mortal sins have turned my soul into a torture room.

I shudder in this park that the winter winds infest
Like Satan's howling laughter while my despair takes bloom
Insanely! While Lord Suicide prepares a tomb! —
To hang myself upon this tree would be the best...
. . . . . . . . . . . . . . . . . . . . . . . . . . . . . . . . . . .
Padre, it's night in town; your prayers I request.

## Notes

LINE 1: *Padre.* The French term is *prêtre* ("priest"), which, when used as a raw form of address, as here, conveys a hint of disdain or at least devaluation. "Padre" is a term available to English that summons a picture of a solicitous yet minimally effective cleric that might console a condemned man's last moments.

LINE 4: *the lowly plebs.* Nelligan says *la plèbe servile* — the servile plebs, which seems an especially gratuitous slur coming from this would-be suicide who declares his life a failure. It might instead be that the poet feels that the will to commit suicide, the grandest sin, a cosmic sin, lifts him above everyone's head. But this is not the only poem where Émile seems to look down upon the lower class, to which, considering his economic circumstances, he belongs. Perhaps he needs to feel distinct from the common run of humanity. Another side of this artistic *hauteur* is in "I Want to Lose Myself" (poem 42), where the poet is grateful to escape his troubled mind by losing himself in the "motley crowd".

LINE 5: *This lonely Town.* The word *Ville* ("Town") was capitalized by Nelligan, which was his adopted style when a word carried extra symbolic weight — for example, as a metaphor for the Self.

LINE 11: *Lord Suicide prepares a tomb!* Nelligan says, *Le suicide aiguise ses coupoirs*, Suicide sharpens its blades.

LINE 12: *To hang myself upon this tree.* The trail of suspension points following this line suggests a pause during which suicide is decided upon.

## Comments

The poet is in a desperate situation. He is possessed by demons and wracked by grievous sins. Here he is next to a hanging tree in a minimally-sketched but plainly wind-tossed park at the eleventh hour confessing to a priest, but with Satan swirling round there looks to be no chance of divine grace breaking through. No words come from the priest.

.../

## Nocturnal Confession

Structurally, the poem is a closed-loop rondel; the tight rhymes and repetitions intensify the sense of entrapment. Historically, the rondel form has musical origins; those repeated lines may be vestiges of a time when proto-rondels as songs were divided between solo and choral voices.

The poet asks the priest to pray for him. It appears the prayers will need to be strong enough to snatch the poet back from the gates of Hell. His sense of guilt is overwhelming. But of what sin is he guilty? Despite the poem's title, the poet does not confess to anything in particular, nor is there any effort to repent, since that would require hope. The crux of the poem is the sense of self-damnation.

What might be the kernel of this sense of guilt? Nowadays we are inclined to look particularly for a sexual component, and it's interesting to note that Nelligan's works include a foreboding poem entitled "Dream on a Hospital Night" which is of uncertain date but has been conjectured to relate to a visit to a psychiatric clinic. While on the premises the poet becomes transfixed by a luminous image of his adored Saint Cecilia, she who conducts the music of Heaven. Suddenly the lights blaze and he hears Saint Cecilia's harp playing. Three lines in the poem are relevant here:

I want no more of sin, I want no more of sex,
For the saint said to me that to hear her music
I need to attend to my salvation on earth.

There's lots of room for speculation as to exactly what kind of sexual experience Nelligan is wracking and damning himself about. We discussed the gay thesis in the Controversies section. There exists also an incest thesis, hinted at in Michel Tremblay's opera *Nelligan* and elsewhere.

In Émile's anguished summer of 1899, so Dantin reported (see Introduction), the poet was tormented by demons and succubae; it's worth noting that this poem's French title, *Confession nocturne,* suggests another phrase known to French, *émission nocturne* — nocturnal emission.

Once again, suicide is at the top of the poet's mind, more imminently now than in "Hypochondriac Nights" (poem 32), and more clearly framed as the only reasonable choice. Suicide is a mortal sin, which will add to the poet's total, but he seems not to be counting.

Were his friends unable to intervene? In summer of 1899, his network of acquaintances seems to have gone into eclipse. Nelligan was no longer participating in the École Littéraire, no longer reciting for the public, no longer seeing his former colleagues. "This lonely Town", he remarks in line 5 of this poem. The young man in this summer of 1899 had two pastimes: he was enrolled in a school for behavioral reform, and he was pouring verses onto his notebooks. A measure of how isolated Nelligan had become is how long it took after his internment on August 9 for his friends to realize that he had disappeared. In December, four months later, not knowing the poet's whereabouts and presumably unable to get useful information from his parents, they published a notice in the journal Les Débats. A colleague requests Monsieur Émile Nelligan to contact the paper, it stated discreetly.

After the poet's tragedy became known, his former colleagues took steps to revive his name before the public. Les Débats was at the forefront, printing a number of Nelligan poems in the years after the internment, and in 1902 publishing an extensive analysis of Nelligan's work by Louis Dantin that trailed across several issues.

~ ~ ~

## 45. The Ship of Gold

A mighty Ship there was, of solid gold 'twas spun,
Its masts touched the sky, it sailed on seas unknown,
While naked Aphrodite, tresses wildly blown,
Reclined along the prow before the blazing sun.

One night upon a hidden reef this vessel tripped
In churning waves enchanted by the Siren's call,
And this awful disaster caused the wreck to fall
Into the deep Abyss, an everlasting crypt.

A Ship of Gold it was, whose see-through side
Exposed a treasure trove for whose possession vied
Neurosis, Hatred and Disgust, those sailor scum.

What's left after the vortex tore at every seam?
That deserted ship, my heart, what next did it become?
Alas! It sank into the endless depths of Dream.

## Notes

LINE 1: *Ship*. This traditional image is recurrent in Nelligan. The ship is his spirit, his hope, his fate. He capitalizes the word to proclaim its symbolic value.

LINE 2: *Its masts touched the sky, it sailed on seas unknown*. This line, in French, is the epitaph on Nelligan's gravestone in Côte de Neiges cemetery in Montréal. The epitaph might alternatively be translated as *his* masts touched the sky, *he* sailed on seas unknown.

LINE 3: *Aphrodite*. Nelligan says *la Cyprine d'amour*, an epithet for Venus-Aphrodite, the ultimate in female desirability, who was born from the sea near Cyprus. Renaissance masters liked to paint her riding the sea on a half-shell.

LINE 4: *Reclined*. The French is *s'étalait*, that is, stretching out on display.

LINE 6: *the Siren's call*. In Greek myth the Sirens are sea nymphs whose sweet song lures mariners to their doom. They are mermaids. Nelligan uses the singular, *la Sirène*, therefore one specific Siren.

LINE 9: *see-through side*. Nelligan says the ship's flanks are *diaphanes*, diaphanous. Yet the ship is made of solid gold. But of course that is *symbolic* gold, ideal gold, fantasy gold. Anyone with eyes to see can discern the convulsions *inside* the vessel.

LINE 14: *the endless depths of Dream*. A premonition of the schizophrenia that will have him institutionalized within a few weeks.

## Comments

This sonnet, composed in the course of summer 1899, is Nelligan's most famous poem — or at least one of the top two, the other being "Wine Song" (poem 37).

Sensual and intensely allegorical, "The Ship of Gold" summarizes the poet's life and predicts an outcome. The poem is Émile at the absolute nerve-end of his craft, spilling out his *cri de cœur* with remorseless logic and not a wasted word.

.../

## The Ship of Gold

The poem did not appear in print until four years after Nelligan's internment. It became the poem his visitors most often asked him to recite.

The poem has a particular resonance in French Canada. Could it be that it triggers a cultural memory? The golden ship plunging into the abyss, does that recall the crash of New France and the loss of the holy Catholic agrarian world?

It's not that simple. *Modern* French Canada might instead appreciate Nelligan's story as the tragedy of their own neurotic poet who went insane in a hyper-Catholic world.

The first quatrain begins boldly. A prodigious sailing ship, sumptuous, cinematic, flies on the wind under the sun. The ship is hewn from solid gold. That is, it is Heaven-born. Nelligan says its masts touch the *azur*, the deep blue sky, the ultimate harmony, the poetic ideal that French poets were known to pursue.

Halfway through the quatrain we suddenly get a different picture. Stretched on the prow is a sex goddess, a Venus-Aphrodite, her naked flesh and windswept hair transmuting the ship into a vector of headlong sensuality. These lines had an erotic flair in Nelligan's time, and even today you can discern it.

Pierre Lemieux (*Nell. am.*) sees "The Ship of Gold" as another poem about the mysterious Gretchen who was Nelligan's Venus as proven by "Gretchen the Pale" (poem 21). The hypothetical Gretchen was, for a time, Émile's lodestar, then there came a coldness between them, and now he has brought her back with a vamped-up image at the tip of his ship.

Behind it all, Nelligan seems to be blaming his breakdown on a pre-Christian sex goddess, a symbol of female beauty, symbol even of the mating principle.

In the second quatrain, it is night. The Ship, enchanted by the Siren's song, strikes a hidden reef. The Siren is the same sort of force as Venus, except with emphasis on the sweet music of deception. The reef? Poet Maurice Rollinat in his poem *L'Amante macabre* wrote that "Life is a ship, for which Evil is the reef".

The third stanza is pathos. Inside the golden Ship, you can see the treasure it carries: the beating heart of a talented poet-to-be. You see as well the riffraff — by name, Disgust, Hatred, and Neurosis — undermining the ship. This is the band of emotions that rage, the switches that flip, within the poet.

The closing stanza is the damage report. The artist is losing his grip on the world, he is a deserted wreck. Venus gone, crew gone. Paris gone. All is lost. We have slipped from the high azure sky to the dark bottom of the ocean. In the last line the poet's heart-ship plummets into the abyss of Dream.

What is that abyss of Dream? We use the word 'dream' in different ways. Someone's hopeful vision of the future is a dream, a spur to action. Dreams may also be uncontrolled sequences scripted by unseen forces, unrolling upon you, speaking to you in symbols, the native language of myth and dream.

It might alternatively be argued that Nelligan's dream was to be a poet who goes insane. This was an archetype a late Romantic poet could aspire to. This was an honorable role if your religion was *l'art pour l'art.* Dantin thought he detected pride in Nelligan's declaration to him that "I will die mad, like Baudelaire".

Émile dreamed of joining the gloried circle of the *poètes maudits,* the heroes of his universe. That ambition, combined with his particular neurology and the realities of his environment, was bound to be trouble. Biographers including Louis Dantin himself concluded that the dream grew so self-convincing that it swallowed the dreamer. In "The Ship of Gold" the poet seems a helpless witness to his own march to dementia.

In a practical sense, the abyss of dream is permanent detachment from reality. Beginning at most a few weeks from writing this verse, Nelligan will spend the rest of his life in mental asylums. "The Ship of Gold" is what Nelligan offers as a self-diagnosis.

~ ~ ~

## 46. The Fool

Gondolar! Gondolar!
On this road you did not get far.

They murdered the poor idiot,
They crushed him beneath a chariot,
Then the dog after the idiot.

They dug them a big, big hole there.
*Dies irae, dies illa.*
On your knees before that hole there!

## Notes

LINE 1: *Gondolar.* A variant, perhaps, of *gondolier.* That would fit with Nelligan's penchant for boating images. French vocabulary additionally has the verb *se gondoler* which primarily means to warp, as wood might warp in the sun; the verb has a secondary meaning, to writhe in laughter.

LINE 7: *Dies irae.* Medieval Latin for Day of Wrath, which would be Judgment Day. Nelligan is alluding to a medieval chant incorporated into the Catholic Mass for the Dead. This then is the doom song that occupies his head at the moment. The relevant sequence is:

> Dies irae, dies illa
> Solvet sæclum in favilla...

which is to say:

> Day of wrath, day when
> The world dissolves into ashes...

## Comments

This poem, which Luc Lacourcière classified among "Fragments" in his 1952 collection (*Poésies Complètes*) of Nelligan's poems, is a vivid illustration of the poet's breakdown in summer of 1899. Gondolar must surely be a name for the poet himself. He is calling to himself at the edge of a precipice.

Let's listen for a moment to some of the prominent words: idiot, murdered, crushed, chariot. The poet is calling himself an idiot and a victim of society at the same time. What does the dog have to do with it? Dogs represent innocent nature; dogs were companions of Émile's pastoral days in poems such as "Watteau Dream" (poem 2) and "Autumn Tarantella" (poem 3).

On August 9, 1899, the poet was taken by carriage to the St.-Benoît asylum in Longue-Pointe; the doctors there pronounced him schizophrenic. In the first months there seem to have been phases when he was out of control and others when he was tranquil.

It may be that treatments were tried on him. Some records have been lost. Nelligan spent the remaining 40-plus years of his life in mental institutions, even as his fame spread in Quebec and his poems were taken up for study in the educational system. Émile is said to have lived in a dreamworld, but he received journalists and literary students and he recited for them. He knew that he counted for something in the real world he had left behind.

~ ~ ~

# Picture Gallery

(1) In March 1899 at age 19 Nelligan sat for this portrait by a professional photographer on rue Saint-Denis. That was a logical career step. But within a few weeks Nelligan went into a tailspin that culminated in his internment in a mental institution. The handwriting is that of painter Charles Gill who was sending a friend this picture of, as he says, "le grand Nelligan", the great Nelligan.

(2) Place Jacques-Cartier in 1900. The journal *Le Monde illustré*, which tracked the local literary scene and published several of Nelligan's poems, had its offices here, overlooking the bustling open-air market in the heart of Vieux Montréal.

(3) Nelligan's first published poem appeared on June 6, 1896 in *Le Samedi*, one of several Montreal journals that supported a burgeoning French-language literary scene.

(4) A modern view (2020) of what was the Nelligan home on avenue Laval, a short distance north of carré Saint-Louis in what is now Montreal's Plateau district. Émile lived here from 1892 to 1899, composing his verses at a desk in his second-floor room with the balcony.

(5) Nelligan circa 1920, age approximately 40, at St.-Benoît asylum. In all, the poet spent forty-two years in mental hospitals.

(6) Rue Saint-Denis, early 20th century. Columnist Robertine Barry lived on this street and held salons on Thursday afternoons. Nelligan would drop by to read poems and borrow the latest reviews from Paris. The relationship suffered a shock when Nelligan declared an amorous interest in Robertine.

(7) Nelligan's fame grew steadily during the 20th century. His life and work were studied in biographies and literary criticism, and he became a subject of works of fiction including film and opera. This Canada postage stamp, issued in 1979, commemorated the centennial of the poet's birth.

(8) *Hommage à Nelligan* by Jean-Paul Lemieux, 1971, here rendered in black and white. The artist seems to link Nelligan's family to the poet's fate, judging by the secretive houses and taking the background figures as one male and three females, which would add up to Nelligan's parents and two sisters.

~~~

Selected Verse of Émile Nelligan

# Appendix

## The source texts

What follows are the French texts upon which I base the translations in this book. Generally I have relied on Nelligan's poems as they appear in the *Poésies complètes 1896-1899* published by La Bibliothèque électronique du Québec, and generally I've followed its styling of the French titles. Since the Bibliothèque's collection includes a few oversights and debatable choices, in a small number of cases I've looked to other places for help: for poems 15, 16, 17, 37 and 42, Réjean Robidoux and Paul Wyczynski, *Émile Nelligan, Poésies Complètes, 1896-1941* (1992); for poems 16, 37 and 38, Louis Dantin, *Émile Nelligan et son Œuvre* (1904); for poem 17, the journal *Le Nationaliste*, March 6, 1904, in the Bibliothèque et Archives nationales du Québec.

### 1. Presque berger

Les Brises ont brui comme des litanies
Et la flute s'exile en molles aphonies.

Les grands bœufs sont rentrés. Ils meuglent dans l'étable
Et la soupe qui fume a réjoui la table.

Fais ta prière, ô Pan ! Allons au lit, mioche,
Que les bras travailleurs se calment de la pioche.

Le clair de lune ondoie aux horizons de soie :
Ô sommeil ! Donnez-moi votre baiser de joie.

Tout est fermé. C'est nuit. Silence… le chien jappe.
Je me couche. Pourtant le songe à mon cœur frappe.

Oui, c'est délicieux, cela, d'être ainsi libre
Et de vivre en berger presque. Un souvenir vibre

En moi… là-bas, au temps de l'enfance, ma vie
Coulait ainsi, loin des sentiers, blanche et ravie !

## 2. Rêve de Watteau

Quand les pastours, aux soirs des crépuscules roux
Menant leurs grands boucs noirs aux râles d'or des flûtes,
Vers le hameau natal, de par delà les buttes,
S'en revenaient, le long des champs piqués de houx ;

Bohèmes écoliers, âmes vierges de luttes,
Pleines de blanc naguère et de jours sans courroux,
En rupture d'étude, aux bois jonchés de brous
Nous allions, gouailleurs, prêtant l'oreille aux chutes

Des ruisseaux, dans le val que longeait en jappant
Le petit chien berger des calmes fils de Pan
Dont le pipeau qui pleure appelle, tout au loin.

Puis, las, nous nous couchions, frissonnants jusqu'aux moelles,
Et parfois, radieux, dans nos palais de foin,
Nous déjeunions d'aurore et nous soupions d'étoiles...

## 3. Tarentelle d'automne

Vois-tu près des cohortes bovines
Choir les feuilles dans les ravines,
    Dans les ravines ?

Vois-tu sur le coteau des années
Choir mes illusions fanées,
    Toutes fanées ?

Avec quelles rageuses prestesses
Court la bise de nos tristesses,
    De mes tristesses !

Vois-tu, près des cohortes bovines,
Choir les feuilles dans les ravines
    Dans les ravines ?

Ma sérénade d'octobre enfle une
Funéraire voix à la lune,
    Au clair de lune.

.../

Avec quelles rageuses prestesses
Court la bise de nos tristesses,
 De mes tristesses !

Le doguet bondit dans la vallée.
Allons-nous-en par cette allée,
 La morne allée !

Ma sérénade d'octobre enfle une
Funéraire voix à la lune,
 Au clair de lune.

On dirait que chaque arbre divorce
Avec sa feuille et son écorce,
 Sa vieille écorce.

Ah ! vois sur la pente des années
Choir mes illusions fanées,
 Toutes fanées !

## 4. Premier remords

Au temps où je portais des habits de velours,
Éparses sur mon col roulaient mes boucles brunes.
J'avais de grands yeux purs comme le clair des lunes;
Dès l'aube je partais, sac au dos, les pas lourds.

Mais en route aussitôt je tramais des détours,
Et, narguant les pions de mes jeunes rancunes,
Je montais à l'assaut des pommes et des prunes
Dans les vergers bordant les murailles des cours.

Étant ainsi resté loin des autres élèves,
Loin des bancs, tout un mois, à vivre au gré des rêves,
Un soir, à la maison, craintif, comme j'entrais,

Devant le crucifix où sa lèvre se colle
Ma mère était en pleurs !... O mes ardents regrets !
Depuis, je fus toujours le premier à l'école.

### 5. Bergère

Vous que j'aimai sous les grands houx,
Aux soirs de bohème champêtre,
Bergère, à la mode champêtre,
De ces soirs vous souvenez-vous ?
Vous étiez l'astre à ma fenêtre
Et l'étoile d'or dans les houx.

Aux soirs de bohème champêtre
Vous que j'aimai sous les grands houx,
Bergère, à la mode champêtre,
Où donc maintenant êtes-vous ?
— Vous êtes l'ombre à ma fenêtre
Et la tristesse dans les houx.

### 6. Violon de villanelle

Sous le clair de lune au frais du vallon
Beaux gars à chefs bruns, belles à chefs blond,
Au son du hautbois ou du violon
　　Dansez la villanelle.

La lande est noyée en des parfums bons.
Attisez la joie au feu des charbons ;
Allez-y gaiement, allez-y par bonds,
　　Dansez la villanelle.

Sur un banc de chêne ils sont là, les vieux,
Vous suivant avec des pleurs dans les yeux,
Lorsqu'en les frôlant vous passez joyeux...
　　Dansez la villanelle.

Allez-y gaiement ! que l'orbe d'argent
Croise sur vos fronts son reflet changeant ;
Bien avant dans la nuit, à la Saint-Jean
　　Dansez la villanelle.

7. *Qu'elle est triste en Octobre*

Qu'elle est triste en Octobre avec sa voix pourprée
    La Vesprée !

Ses funéraires las ! enamourent les choses
    Trop moroses.

En chambre rose et blanche une vierge repose
    Blanche et rose.

Et le hameau se tait. Les bergers qui reviennent
    Se souviennent

Dans la marche des monts parmi le ranz des sources
    De ses courses

D'autrefois avec eux. Archange bucolique
    Ô relique

D'enfance à jamais douce ! Un d'entre eux là ne parle.
    C'est Fritz. Car le

Vieux chevrier, le roi des chèvres vagabondes
    Près des ondes,

L'aima. Qu'il la déplore ! Il était son égide
    Bloc rigide

Contre lequel les Temps avaient usé leur lime.
    Le sublime

Vieillard pleurait sa mort comme une fleur de neige.
    Un cortège

S'est formé. Deux bras lourds l'amènent en chapelle.
    Une pelle

Dans le souterrain creuse un exil de la vie
    Qu'ont suivie

Tous mes pas douloureux. Elle gît là en terre,
    Solitaire.

Je l'entends dans mon rêve. Elle pleure en les cloches
    Aux approches

.../

Du soir. J'ai gardé d'elle un souvenir de frère,
  Lutte chère

Avec l'autre d'antan. Chez moi, douleur n'est fraîche,
  Elle est sèche

De ce feu qui l'embrase en ses rouges fournaises
  Dans les braises.

Douleur où j'ai tant soif que je boirais les mondes
  Et leurs ondes.

Douleur où je péris comme un lys sur console
  Sans parole...

Qu'elle est triste en Octobre avec sa voix pourprée
  La Vesprée !

## 8. Aubade rouge

L'aube éclabousse les monts de sang
  Tout drapés de fine brume,

Et l'on entend meugler frémissant
  Un bœuf au naseau qui fume.

Voici l'heure de la boucherie.
  Le tenant par son licol,

Les gars pour la prochaine tuerie
  Ont mis le mouchoir au col.

La hache s'abat avec tel han,
  Qu'ils pausent contre habitude.

*Procumbit bos.* Tel un éléphant
  Croule en une solitude.

Le sang gicle. Il laboure des cornes
  Le sol teint rouge hideux

Et Phébus chante aux beuglements mornes
  Du bœuf qu'on rupture à deux.

### 9. Moines en défilade

Ils défilent le long des corridors antiques,
Tête basse, égrenant d'énormes chapelets ;
Et le soir qui s'en vient, du sang de ses reflets
Empourpre la splendeur des dalles monastiques.

L'heure a versé déjà ses flammes extatiques
Au fond de leurs grands cœurs où bouillent les secrets
De leur dégoût humain, de leurs mornes regrets,
Et du frisson dompté des chairs cénobitiques.

Ils marchent dans la nuit et rien ne les émeut,
Pas même l'effrayante, horrible ombre du feu
Qui les suit sur le mur jusqu'au seuil des chapelles,

Pas même les appels de l'infernal esprit,
Suprême Tentateur des passions rebelles
De ces silencieux Spectres de Jésus-Christ.

### 10. Paysage fauve

Les arbres comme autant de vieillards rachitiques,
Flanqués vers l'horizon sur les escarpements,
Ainsi que des damnés sous le fouet des tourments,
Tordent de désespoir leurs torses fantastiques.

C'est l'Hiver ; c'est la Mort ; sur les neiges arctiques,
Vers le bucher qui flambe aux lointains campements,
Les chasseurs vont frileux sous leurs lourds vêtements,
Et galopent, fouettant leurs chevaux athlétiques.

La bise hurle ; il grêle ; il fait nuit, tout est sombre ;
Et voici que soudain se dessine dans l'ombre
Un farouche troupeau de grands loups affamés ;

Ils bondissent, essaims de fauves multitudes,
Et la brutale horreur de leurs yeux enflammés
Allume de points d'or les blanches solitudes.

## 11. Devant deux portraits de ma mère

Ma mère, que je l'aime en ce portrait ancien,
Peint aux jours glorieux qu'elle était jeune fille,
Le front couleur de lys et le regard qui brille
Comme un éblouissant miroir vénitien !

Ma mère que voici n'est plus du tout la même ;
Les rides ont creusé le beau marbre frontal ;
Elle a perdu l'éclat du temps sentimental
Où son hymen chanta comme un rose poème.

Aujourd'hui je compare, et j'en suis triste aussi,
Ce front nimbé de joie et ce front de souci,
Soleil d'or, brouillard dense au couchant des années.

Mais, mystère de cœur qui ne peut s'éclairer !
Comment puis-je sourire à ces lèvres fanées ?
Au portrait qui sourit, comment puis-je pleurer ?

## 12. Clair de lune intellectuel

Ma pensée est couleur de lumières lointaines,
Du fond de quelque crypte aux vagues profondeurs.
Elle a l'éclat parfois des subtiles verdeurs
D'un golfe où le soleil abaisse ses antennes.

En un jardin sonore, au soupir des fontaines,
Elle a vécu dans les soirs doux, dans les odeurs;
Ma pensée est couleur de lumières lointaines,
Du fond de quelque crypte aux vagues profondeurs.

Elle court à jamais les blanches prétentaines,
Au pays angélique où montent ses ardeurs,
Et, loin de la matière et des brutes laideurs,
Elle rêve l'essor aux célestes Athènes.

Ma pensée est couleur de lunes d'or lointaines.

### 13. Les vieilles rues

Que vous disent les vieilles rues
    Des vieilles cités ?...
Parmi les poussières accrues
    De leurs vétustés,
Rêvant de choses disparues,
Que vous disent les vieilles rues ?

Alors que vous y marchez tard
    Pour leur rendre hommage :
— « De plus d'une âme de vieillard
    Nous sommes l'image, »
Disent-elles dans le brouillard,
Alors que vous y marchez tard.

« Comme d'anciens passants nocturnes
    « Qui longent nos murs,
« En eux ayant les noires urnes
    « De leurs ans impurs,
« S'en vont les Remords taciturnes
« Comme d'anciens passants nocturnes. »

Voilà ce que dans les cités
    Maintes vieilles rues
Disent parmi les vétustés
    Des choses accrues
Parmi vos gloires disparues,
O mornes et mortes cités !

### 14. Marches funèbres

J'écoute en moi des voix funèbres
Clamer transcendentalement,
Quand sur un motif allemand
Se rythment ces marches célèbres.

Au frisson fou de mes vertèbres
Si je sanglote éperdument,
C'est que j'entends des voix funèbres
Clamer transcendentalement.

.../

Tel un troupeau spectral de zèbres
Mon rêve rôde étrangement ;
Et je suis hanté tellement
Qu'en moi toujours, dans mes ténèbres,

J'entends geindre des voix funèbres.

## 15. La Sorella dell' Amore

Mort, que fais-tu, dis-nous, de tous ces beaux trophées
De vierges que nos feux brûlent sur tes autels ?
Réponds, quand serons-nous pour jamais immortels
Aux lumineux séjours des célestes Riphées ?

J'eus vécu l'Idéal. Au paradis des Fées
Elle était !... Je ne sais, mais elle avait de tels
Yeux que j'y voyais poindre, aux soirs, de grands castels
Massifs d'orgueil parmi des parcs et des nymphées...

Ma chère, il est vesprée, allons par bois, viens-t'en
Nous suivrons tous les deux le chemin brut et rude
Que tu sais adjoignant la chapelle d'Antan.

Ma voix t'appelle, ô sœur ! mais ta voix d'or m'élude.
Lucile est morte hier et je sanglote étant
Comme une cloche vaine en une solitude.

## 16. Placet

Reine, acquiescez-vous qu'une boucle déferle
Des lames de cheveux aux lames du ciseau,
Pour que j'y puisse humer un peu de chant d'oiseau,
Un peu de soir d'amour né de vos yeux de perle?

Au bosquet de mon cœur, en des trilles de merle,
Votre âme a fait chanter sa flûte de roseau.
Reine, acquiescez-vous qu'une boucle déferle
Des lames des cheveux aux lames du ciseau?

Fleur soyeuse aux parfums de rose, lis ou berle,
Je vous la remettrai, secrète comme un sceau,
Fût-ce en Éden, au jour que nous prendrons vaisseau
Sur la mer idéale où l'ouragan se ferle.

Reine, acquiescez-vous qu'une boucle déferle?

*17. Sur un portrait de Dante*

C'est lui, le pèlerin de l'ombre revenu,
Au front noirci du hâle infernal de l'abîme,
À l'œil où flotte encor la vision sublime,
L'artiste incomparable et l'homme méconnu.

Loin des fourbes jaloux dont il fut la victime,
Après avoir montré leur âme immonde à nu,
Des monts olympiens il a touché la cime
Et retrouvé la paix de son rêve ingénu.

Ô Dante Alighieri, gardien des cimetières !
Le blason glorieux de tes œuvres altières
Au mur des sages brille, ineffaçable et fier !

Et tu vivras aussi longtemps que Dieu lui-même,
Car le Ciel éternel et l'éternel Enfer
Ont appris les accents de ton ardent poème.

*18. L'ultimo angelo del Correggio*

Les yeux hagards, la joue pâlie,
Mais le cœur ferme et sans regret,
Dans sa mansarde d'Italie
Le divin Corrège expirait.

Autour de l'atroce grabat,
La bonne famille du maître
Cherche un peu de sa vie à mettre
Dans son cœur à peine qui bat.

Mais la vision cérébrale
Fomente la fièvre du corps,
Et son âme qu'agite un râle,
Sonne de bizarres accords.

Il veut peindre. Très lentement
De l'oreiller il se soulève,
Simulant quelque archange en rêve
En oubli du Ciel un moment.

.../

Son œil fouille la chambre toute,
Et soudain se fixe, étonné.
Il voit son modèle, il n'a doute,
Dans le berceau du dernier né.

Son jeune enfant près du panneau
Tout rose dans le linge orange,
A joint ses petites mains d'ange
Vers le cadre du Bambino.

Et sa filiale prière
À celle de l'Éden fait lien :
Dans du soir d'or italien,
Vision de blanche lumière.

« Vite qu'on m'apporte un pinceau !
« Mes couleurs ! crie le vieil artiste,
« Je veux peindre la pose triste
« De mon enfant dans son berceau.

« Mon pinceau ! délire Corrège,
« Je veux saisir en son essor
« Ce sublime idéal de neige
« Avant qu'il retourne au ciel d'or ! »

Comme il peint ! Comme sur la toile
Le génie coule à flot profond !
C'est un chérubin au chef blond,
En chemise couleur d'étoile.

Mais le peintre, pris tout à coup
D'un hoquet, retombe. Il expire.
Tandis que la sueur au cou
S'est figée en perles de cire.

Ainsi mourut l'artiste étrange
Dont le cœur d'idéal fut plein ;
Qui fit de son enfant un ange,
Avant d'en faire un orphelin.

## 19. Sonnet d'or

Dans le soir triomphal la froidure agonise
Et les frissons divins du printemps ont surgi ;
L'Hiver n'est plus, vivat ! car l'Avril bostangi,
Du grand sérail de Flore a repris la maîtrise.

Certe, ouvre la persienne, et que cet air qui grise,
Se mêlant aux reflets d'un ciel pur et rougi,
Rôde dans le boudoir où notre amour régit
Avec les sons mourants que ton luth improvise.

Allègre, Yvette, allègre, et crois-moi : j'aime mieux
Me griser du chant d'or de ces oiseaux joyeux,
Que d'entendre gémir ton grand clavier d'ivoire.

Allons rêver au parc verdi sous le dégel :
Et là tu me diras si leur Avril de gloire
Ne vaut pas en effet tout Mozart et Haendel.

## 20. Sieste ecclésiastique

*Croquis d'été*

Vraiment, il a bel air sous sa neuve soutane,
Ce cher petit abbé, joufflu, rasé tout frais,
Pour qui la bonne table a d'innocents attraits...
Il en rêve au couvert de l'ombrageux platane.

Midi sonne. En plein ciel le soleil se pavane,
Et monsieur le vicaire, ô scandaleux portrait !
S'est endormi, tout rond, sur la pelouse, abstrait,
Songeant aux gros péchés de quelque courtisane.

On vient de la cuisine... et, sous le blanc rideau,
Blanche pousse Michel, Louise, le bedeau,
Et tous de s'esquiver en éclatant de rire,

Cependant que l'abbé, ne se reprochant rien,
S'étire et murmure en un céleste sourire
Que Bacchus, après tout, était un bon chrétien.

### 21. *Gretchen la pâle*

Elle est de la beauté des profils de Rubens
Dont la majesté calme à la sienne s'incline.
Sa voix a le son d'or de mainte mandoline
Aux balcons de Venise avec des chants lambins.

Ses cheveux, en des flots lumineux d'eaux de bains,
Déferlent sur sa chair vierge de manteline ;
Son pas, soupir lacté de fraîche mousseline,
Simule un vespéral marcher de chérubins.

Elle est comme de l'or d'une blondeur étrange.
Vient-elle de l'Éden ? De l'Érèbe ? Est-ce un ange
Que ce mystérieux chef-d'œuvre du limon ?

La voilà se dressant, torse, comme un jeune arbre.
Souple Anadyomène… Ah ! gare à ce démon !
C'est le Paros qui tue avec ses bras de marbre !

### 22. *Frère Alfus, première partie*

Ce fut un homme chaste, humble, doux et savant
Que le vieux frère Alfus, le moine des légendes.
Il vivait à Olmutz dans un ancien couvent.

Il avait un renom de par beaucoup de landes,
Son esprit était plein d'un immense savoir
Car la Science lui fit ses insignes offrandes.

De tous bords l'on venait pour l'aimer et le voir ;
Son chef s'était blanchi sous des frimas d'idées
Mais son penser restait sur un point sans pouvoir.

Parmi les grandes paix des retraites sondées,
Dès l'aube, tout rêveur il venait là souvent
Quand les herbes chantaient sous les primes ondées.

Il écoutait la source et l'oiseau, puis le vent,
Et comme en désespoir de solver le mystère
Il retournait pensif toujours vers son couvent.

…/

On le vit se voûter comme l'arbre au parterre.
Peu à peu dans son âme une tempête entra
Car le Doute y grondait comme un rauque cratère.

Du glaive de l'orgueil l'humble foi s'éventra
Et le vieux moine allait portant sur ses épaules
Les douleurs que l'enfer sans doute y concentra.

Parfois il se disait marchant sous les hauts saules,
L'index contre la tempe et le missel au bras,
Dieu peut-être est chimère ainsi que vains nos rôles.

À quoi nous servirait ainsi jusqu'au trépas
De cambrer nos désirs sous les cilices chastes
Et vivre en pleine mort pour un ciel qui n'est pas ?

Son cœur confabulait avec des voix néfastes,
Le ciel, l'arbre, l'oiseau, la terre étaient joyeux
Et le Moine était triste au fond de ces bois vastes.


### 23. Les petits oiseaux

Puisque Rusbrock m'enseigne
À moi, dont le cœur saigne
Sur tout ce qui se baigne
    Dans le malheur,
À vous aimer, j'élève
Ma pensée à ce rêve :
De vous faire une grève
    Avec mon cœur.

Là donc, oiseaux sauvages,
Contre tous les ravages,
Vous aurez vos rivages
    Et vos abris :
Colombes, hirondelles,
Entre mes mains fidèles,
Oiseaux aux clairs coups d'ailes,
    Ô colibris !

.../

Sûrs vous pourrez y vivre
Sans peur des soirs de givre
Où sous l'astre de cuivre,
    Morne flambeau !
Souventes fois, cortège
Qu'un vent trop dur assiège,
Vous trouvez sous la neige
    Votre tombeau.

Protégés sans relâche,
Ainsi contre un plomb lâche,
Quand je clorai ma tâche,
    Membres raidis ;
Vous, par l'immense voûte
Me guiderez sans doute,
Connaissant mieux la route
    Du Paradis !

## 24. Sainte Cécile

La belle Sainte au fond des cieux
Mène l'orchestre archangélique,
Dans la lointaine basilique
Dont la splendeur hante mes yeux.

Depuis que la Vierge biblique
Lui légua ce poste pieux,
La belle Sainte au fond des cieux,
Mène l'orchestre archangélique.

Loin du monde diabolique
Puissé-je un soir mystérieux,
Ouïr, dans les divins milieux
Ton clavecin mélancolique,

Ma belle Sainte, au fond des cieux.

### 25. La cloche dans la brume

Écoutez, écoutez, ô ma pauvre âme ! Il pleure
Tout au loin dans la brume ! Une cloche ! Des sons
Gémissent sous le noir des nocturnes frissons,
Pendant qu'une tristesse immense nous effleure.

À quoi songez-vous donc ? à quoi pensez-vous tant ?...
Vous qui ne priez plus, ah ! serait-ce, pauvresse,
Que vous compareriez soudain votre détresse
À la cloche qui rêve aux angélus d'antan ?...

Comme elle vous geignez, funèbre et monotone,
Comme elle vous tintez dans les brouillards d'automne,
Plainte de quelque église exilée en la nuit,

Et qui regrette avec de sonores souffrances
Les fidèles quittant son enceinte qui luit,
Comme vous regrettez l'exil des Espérances.

### 26. Christ en croix

Je remarquais toujours ce grand Jésus de plâtre
Dressé comme un pardon au seuil du vieux couvent,
Échafaud solennel à geste noir, devant
Lequel je me courbais, saintement idolâtre.

Or, l'autre soir, à l'heure où le cri-cri folâtre,
Par les prés assombris, le regard bleu rêvant,
Récitant Éloa, les cheveux dans le vent,
Comme il sied à l'Éphèbe esthétique et bellâtre,

J'aperçus, adjoignant des débris de parois,
Un gigantesque amas de lourde vieille croix
Et de plâtre écroulé parmi les primevères ;

Et je restai là, morne, avec les yeux pensifs,
Et j'entendais en moi des marteaux convulsifs
Renforcer les clous noirs des intimes Calvaires !

### 27. Roses d'octobre

Pour ne pas voir choir les roses d'automne,
Cloître ton cœur mort en mon cœur tué.
Vers des soirs souffrants mon deuil s'est rué,
Parallèlement au mois monotone.

Le carmin tardif et joyeux détonne
Sur le bois dolent de roux ponctué...
Pour ne pas voir choir les roses d'automne,
Cloître ton cœur mort en mon cœur tué.

Là-bas, les cyprès ont l'aspect atone ;
À leur ombre on est vite habitué,
Sous terre un lit frais s'ouvre situé ;
Nous y dormirons tous deux, ma mignonne,

Pour ne pas voir choir les roses d'automne.

### 28. Soir d'hiver

Ah ! comme la neige a neigé !
Ma vitre est un jardin de givre.
Ah ! comme la neige a neigé !
Qu'est-ce que le spasme de vivre
À la douleur que j'ai, que j'ai !

Tous les étangs gisent gelés,
Mon âme est noire : Où vis-je? où vais-je?
Tous ses espoirs gisent gelés :
Je suis la nouvelle Norvège
D'où les blonds ciels s'en sont allés.

Pleurez, oiseaux de février,
Au sinistre frisson des choses,
Pleurez, oiseaux de février,
Pleurez mes pleurs, pleurez mes roses,
Aux branches du genévrier.

Ah ! comme la neige a neigé !
Ma vitre est un jardin de givre.
Ah ! comme la neige a neigé !
Qu'est-ce que le spasme de vivre
À tout l'ennui que j'ai, que j'ai !...

### 29. Un poète

Laissez-le vivre ainsi sans lui faire de mal !
Laissez-le s'en aller, c'est un rêveur qui passe ;
C'est une âme angélique ouverte sur l'espace,
Qui porte en elle un ciel de printemps auroral.

C'est une poésie aussi triste que pure
Qui s'élève de lui dans un tourbillon d'or.
L'étiole la comprend, l'étoile qui s'endort
Dans sa blancheur céleste aux frissons de guipure.

Il ne veut rien savoir ; il aime sans amour.
Ne le regardez pas ! Que nul ne s'en occupe !
Dites même qu'il est de son propre sort dupe !
Riez de lui !... Qu'importe ! Il faut mourir un jour…

Alors, dans le pays où le bon Dieu demeure,
On vous fera connaître, avec reproche amer,
Ce qu'il fut de candeur sous ce front simple et fier
Et de tristesse dans ce grand œil gris qui pleure !

### 30. Rondel à ma pipe

Les pieds sur les chenets de fer
Devant un bock, ma bonne pipe,
Selon notre amical principe
Rêvons à deux, ce soir d'hiver.

Puisque le ciel me prend en grippe
(N'ai-je pourtant assez souffert ?)
Les pieds sur les chenets de fer
Devant un bock rêvons, ma pipe.

Preste, la mort que j'anticipe
Va me tirer de cet enfer
Pour celui du vieux Lucifer ;
Soit ! nous fumerons chez ce type,

Les pieds sur les chenets de fer.

*31. Le bœuf spectral*

Le grand bœuf roux aux cornes glauques
Hante là-bas la paix des champs,
Et va meuglant dans les couchants
Horriblement ses râles rauques.

Et tous ont tu leurs gais colloques
Sous l'orme au soir avec leurs chants.
Le grand bœuf roux aux cornes glauque
Hante là-bas la paix des champs.

Gare, gare aux desseins méchants !
Belles en blanc, vachers en loques,
Prenez à votre cou vos socques !
À travers prés, buissons tranchants,

Fuyez le bœuf aux cornes glauques.

*32. Soirs hypocondriaques*

Parfois je prends mon front blêmi
Sous des impulsions tragiques
Quand le clavecin a frémi,

Et que les lustres léthargiques
Plaquent leurs rayons sur mon deuil
Avec les sons noirs des musiques.

Et les pleurs mal cachés dans l'œil
Je cours affolé par les chambres
Trouvant partout que triste accueil ;

Et de grands froids glacent mes membres :
Je cherche à me suicider
Par vos soirs affreux, ô Décembres !

Anges maudits, veuillez m'aider !

### 33. Notre-Dame-des-Neiges

Sainte Notre-Dame, en beau manteau d'or,
    De sa lande fleurie
Descend chaque soir, quand son Jésus dort
    En sa Ville-Marie.
Sous l'astral flambeau que portent ses anges,
    La belle Vierge va
Triomphalement, aux accords étranges
    De céleste bîva.

Sainte Notre-Dame a là-haut son trône
    Sur notre Mont-Royal ;
Et de là, son œil subjugue le Faune
    De l'abîme infernal.
Car elle a dicté : « Qu'un ange protège
    De son arme de feu
Ma ville d'argent au collier de neige »,
    La Dame du Ciel bleu !

Sainte Notre-Dame, ô tôt nous délivre
    De tout joug pour le tien ;
Chasse l'étranger ! Au pays de givre
    Sois-nous force et soutien.
Ce placet fleuri de choses dorées,
    Puisses-tu de tes yeux,
Bénigne, le lire aux roses vesprées,
    Quand tu nous viens des Cieux !

Sainte Notre-Dame a pleuré longtemps
    Parmi ses petits anges ;
Tellement, dit-on, qu'en les cieux latents
    Se font des bruits étranges,
Et que notre Vierge entraînant l'Éden,
    Ô floraison chérie !
Va tôt refleurir en même jardin
    Sa France et sa Ville-Marie ...

### 34. Amour immaculé

Je sais en une église un vitrail merveilleux
Où quelque artiste illustre, inspiré des archanges,
A peint d'une façon mystique, en robe à franges,
Le front nimbé d'un astre, une Sainte aux yeux bleus.

Le soir, l'esprit hanté de rêves nébuleux
Et du céleste écho de récitals étranges,
Je m'en viens la prier sous les lueurs oranges
De la lune qui luit entre ses blonds cheveux.

Telle sur le vitrail de mon cœur je t'ai peinte,
Ma romanesque aimée, ô pâle et blonde sainte,
Toi, la seule que j'aime et toujours aimerai ;

Mais tu restes muette, impassible, et, trop fière,
Tu te plais à me voir, sombre et désespéré,
Errer dans mon amour comme en un cimetière !


### 35. Le tombeau de la négresse

Après que nous eut fui le grand vent des hivers,
Aux derniers ciels pâlis de mars, nous la menâmes
Dans le hallier funèbre aux odeurs de cinnames,
Où germaient les soupçons de nouveaux plants rouverts.

De hauts rameaux étaient criblés d'oiseaux divers
Et de tristes soupirs gonflaient leurs jeunes âmes.
Au limon moite et brut où nous la retournâmes,
Que l'Africaine dorme en paix dans les mois verts !

Le sol pieusement recouvrira ses planches ;
Et le bon bengali, dans son château de branches,
Pleurera sur maint thème un peu de ses vingt ans.

Peut-être, revenus en un lointain printemps,
Verrons-nous, de son cœur, dans les buissons latents,
Éclore un grand lys noir entre des roses blanches.

## 36. Le Robin des bois

Pendant que nous lisions Werther au fond des bois,
Hier s'en vint chanter un robin dans les branches ;
Et j'ai saisi vos mains, j'ai saisi vos mains blanches,
Et je vous ai parlé d'amour comme autrefois.

Mais vous êtes restée insensible à ma voix,
Muette au jeune aveu des affections franches ;
Quand soudain, vous levant, courant dans les pervenches,
Émue, et m'appelant, vous m'avez crié : « Vois ! »

Voici qu'était tombé du frissonnant feuillage
L'oiseau sentimental, frappé dans son jeune âge,
Et qui mourait sitôt, pauvre ami du printemps.

Et vous, vous le pleuriez, regrettant sa romance,
Pendant que je songeais, fixant l'azur immense :
Le Robin et l'Amour ont morts en même temps !

## 37. La romance du vin

Tout se mêle en un vif éclat de gaîté verte.
Ô le beau soir de mai ! Tous les oiseaux en chœur,
Ainsi que les espoirs naguères à mon cœur,
Modulent leur prélude à ma croisée ouverte.

Ô le beau soir de mai ! le joyeux soir de mai !
Un orgue au loin éclate en froides mélopées ;
Et les rayons, ainsi que de pourpres épées,
Percent le cœur du jour qui se meurt parfumé.

Je suis gai ! je suis gai ! Dans le cristal qui chante,
Verse, verse le vin ! verse encore et toujours,
Que je puisse oublier la tristesse des jours,
Dans le dédain que j'ai de la foule méchante !

Je suis gai ! je suis gai ! Vive le vin et l'Art !...
J'ai le rêve de faire aussi des vers célèbres,
Des vers qui gémiront les musiques funèbres
Des vents d'automne au loin passant dans le brouillard.

C'est le règne du rire amer et de la rage
De se savoir poète et l'objet du mépris,

.../

De se savoir un cœur et de n'être compris
Que par le clair de lune et les grands soirs d'orage !

Femmes ! je bois à vous qui riez du chemin
Où l'idéal m'appelle en ouvrant ses bras roses ;
Je bois à vous surtout, hommes aux fronts moroses
Qui dédaignez ma vie et repoussez ma main !

Pendant que tout l'azur s'étoile dans la gloire,
Et qu'un hymne s'entonne au renouveau doré,
Sur le jour expirant je n'ai donc pas pleuré,
Moi qui marche à tâtons dans ma jeunesse noire !

Je suis gai ! je suis gai ! Vive le soir de mai !
Je suis follement gai, sans être pourtant ivre !...
Serait-ce que je suis enfin heureux de vivre ;
Enfin mon cœur est-il guéri d'avoir aimé ?

Les cloches ont chanté ; le vent du soir odore...
Et pendant que le vin ruisselle à joyeux flots,
Je suis si gai, si gai, dans mon rire sonore,
Oh ! si gai, que j'ai peur d'éclater en sanglots !

## 38. Le puits hanté

Dans le puits noir que tu vois là
Gît la source de tout ce drame.
Aux vents du soir le cerf qui brame
Parmi les bois conte cela.

Jadis un amant fou, voilà,
Y fut noyé par une femme.
Dans le puits noir que tu vois là
Gît la source de tout ce drame.

Pstt ! n'y viens pas ! On voit l'éclat
Mystérieux d'un spectre en flamme,
Et l'on entend, la nuit, une âme
Râler comme en affreux gala,

Dans le puits noir que tu vois là.

## 39. La Vierge noire

Elle a les yeux pareils à d'étranges flambeaux
Et ses cheveux d'or faux sur ses maigres épaules,
Dans des subtils frissons de feuillages de saules,
L'habillent comme font les cyprès des tombeaux.

Elle porte toujours ses robes par lambeaux,
Elle est noire et méchante ; or qu'on la mette aux geôles,
Qu'on la batte à jamais à grands fouets de tôles.
Gare d'elle, mortels, c'est la chair des corbeaux !

Elle m'avait souri d'une bonté profonde,
Je l'aurais crue aimable et, sans souci du monde,
Nous nous serions tenus, Elle et moi par les mains.

Mais, quand je lui parlai, le regard noir d'envie,
Elle me dit : tes pas ont souillé mes chemins.
Certes, tu la connais, on l'appelle la Vie !

## 40. Châteaux en Espagne

Je rêve de marcher comme un conquistador,
Haussant mon labarum triomphal de victoire,
Plein de fierté farouche et de valeur notoire,
Vers des assauts de ville aux tours de bronze et d'or.

Comme un royal oiseau, vautour, aigle ou condor,
Je rêve de planer au divin territoire,
De brûler au soleil mes deux ailes de gloire
À vouloir dérober le céleste Trésor.

Je ne suis hospodar, ni grand oiseau de proie ;
À peine si je puis dans mon cœur qui guerroie
Soutenir le combat des vieux Anges impurs ;

Et mes rêves altiers fondent comme des cierges
Devant cette Ilion éternelle aux cent murs,
La ville de l'Amour imprenable des Vierges !

### 41. *Potiche*

C'est un vase d'Égypte à riche ciselure,
Où sont peints des sphinx bleus et des lions ambrés :
De profil on y voit, souple, les reins cambrés,
Une immobile Isis tordant sa chevelure.

Flambantes, des nefs d'or se glissent sans voilure
Sur une eau d'argent plane aux tons de ciel marbrés :
C'est un vase d'Égypte à riche ciselure
Où sont peints des sphinx bleus et des lions ambrés.

Mon âme est une potiche où pleurent, dédorés,
De vieux espoirs mal peints sur sa fausse moulure ;
Aussi j'en souffre en moi comme d'une brûlure,
Mais le trépas bientôt les aura tous sabrés...

Car ma vie est un vase à pauvre ciselure.

### 42. *Je veux m'éluder*

Je veux m'éluder dans les rires,
Dans des tourbes de gaîté brusque.
Oui, je voudrais me tromper jusque
En des ouragans de délires.

Pitié ! quels monstrueux vampires
Vont suçant mon cœur qui s'offusque !
Ô je veux être fou, ne fût-ce que
Pour narguer mes Détresses pires !

Lent comme un monstre cadavre,
Mon cœur vaisseau s'amarre au havre
De toute hétéromorphe engeance.

Que je bénis ces gueux de rosses
Dont les hilarités féroces
Raillent la vierge Intelligence !

### 43. Les corbeaux

J'ai cru voir sur mon cœur un essaim de corbeaux
En pleine lande intime avec des vols funèbres,
De grands corbeaux venus de montagnes célèbres
Et qui passaient au clair de lune et de flambeaux.

Lugubrement, comme en cercle sur des tombeaux
Et flairant un régal de carcasses de zèbres,
Ils planaient au frisson glacé de mes vertèbres,
Agitant à leurs becs une chair en lambeaux.

Or, cette proie échue à ces démons des nuits
N'était autre que ma Vie en loque, aux ennuis
Vastes qui vont tournant sur elle ainsi toujours,

Déchirant à large coups de bec, sans quartier,
Mon âme, une charogne éparse au champ des jours,
Que ces vieux corbeaux dévoreront en entier.

### 44. Confession nocturne

Prêtre, je suis hanté, c'est la nuit dans la ville,
Mon âme est le donjon des mortels péchés noirs,
Il pleut une tristesse horrible aux promenoirs
Et personne ne vient de la plèbe servile.

Tout est calme et tout dort. La solitaire Ville
S'aggrave de l'horreur vaste des vieux manoirs.
Prêtre, je suis hanté, c'est la nuit dans la ville ;
Mon âme est le donjon des mortels péchés noirs.

En le parc hivernal sous la bise incivile,
Lucifer rôde et va raillant mes désespoirs
Très fous !...Le suicide aiguise ses coupoirs !
Pour se pendre, il fait bon sous cet arbre tranquille…
…………………………………………………………
Prêtre, priez pour moi, c'est la nuit dans la ville.

## 45. Le vaisseau d'or

Ce fut un grand Vaisseau taillé dans l'or massif :
Ses mâts touchaient l'azur, sur des mers inconnues ;
La Cyprine d'amour, cheveux épars, chairs nues,
S'étalait à sa proue, au soleil excessif.

Mais il vint une nuit frapper le grand écueil
Dans l'Océan trompeur où chantait la Sirène,
Et le naufrage horrible inclina sa carène
Aux profondeurs du Gouffre, immuable cercueil.

Ce fut un Vaisseau d'Or, dont les flancs diaphanes
Révélaient des trésors que les marins profanes,
Dégoût, Haine et Névrose, entre eux ont disputés.

Que reste-t-il de lui dans la tempête brève ?
Qu'est devenu mon cœur, navire déserté ?
Hélas ! Il a sombré dans l'abîme du Rêve !

## 46. Le fou

Gondolar ! Gondolar !
Tu n'es plus sur le chemin très tard.

On assassina l'pauvre idiot,
On l'écrasa sous un chariot,
Et puis l'chien après l'idiot.

On leur fit un grand, grand trou là.
Dies irae, dies illa.
À genoux devant ce trou-là !

~~~

## Index des titres de poèmes en français

# Picture references

Picture Gallery 1
1899 portrait
https://crccf.uottawa.ca/exposition_virtuelle/collection_fonds_archives/docu
ment.php?id=387 Photo : Laprés & Lavergne. Université d'Ottawa, CRCCF,
Fonds Paul-Wyczynski (P19), Ph29-23/1.
« Émile Nelligan, au début de 1899. Photographie dédicacée par Charles Gill
et offerte à Albert Lozeau : « À mon ami Albert Lozeau, ce portrait du grand
Nelligan. Tous trois, nous avons adoré la Poésie ; nous l'avons adorée,
puisqu'elle est divine. Est-ce pour cela que nos trois noms se rencontrent là, ou
bien est-ce parce que le malheur nous a frappés tous trois. ? »

Picture Gallery 2
Place Jacques-Cartier
https://commons.wikimedia.org/wiki/File:Montreal_Jacques_Cartier_Square_
1900_LOC_4a08028u.jpg#filehistory
Jacques Cartier Square, Montreal ca.1900. Photographer: William Henry
Jackson, 1843-1942. Detroit Publishing Co., publisher.

Picture Gallery 3
*Le Samedi* cover
*Le Samedi* Vol. 8, no 1 (6 juin 1896)
Montréal : Poirier, Bessette & Cie, (1896)
https://www.canadiana.ca/view/oocihm.8_06319_366/2?r=0&s=1

Picture Gallery 4
The Nelligan house in Montreal
Source: Google Street View, 2020
https://www.google.ca/maps/place/3958+Av.+Laval,+Montreal

Picture Gallery 5
Nelligan circa 1920, age approximately 40…
https://ville.montreal.qc.ca/memoiresdesmontrealais/files/emile-nelligan-en-1920
« Émile Nelligan à l'asile Saint-Benoît-Joseph-Labre, Montréal. »
photographed by Joseph-Octave Lagacé, Université d'Ottawa, Fonds Paul-Wyczynski; located on ville.montreal.qc.ca 1920, Émile Nelligan à l'asile Saint-Benoît-Joseph-Labre, Montréal, par Joseph-Octave Lagacé, Université d'Ottawa, CRCCF, Fonds Paul-Wyczynski (P19), Ph29-7.

Picture Gallery 6
Rue Saint-Denis
https://ville.montreal.qc.ca/memoiresdesmontrealais/files/tramway-rue-saint-denis
« Tramway sur la rue Saint-Denis. » Photographer: Edgar Gariépy, 1914.
Archives de la Ville de Montréal, BM42-G1227

Picture Gallery 7
Postage stamp, 1979. Monique Charbonneau designed the woodcut illustration using the Japanese inking technique called ukiyo-e.
https://www.stampsandcanada.com/stamps-prices-canada-stamp.php?postage=emile-nelligan-le-vaisseau-d-or&denomination=17-cents&stamp=751&cat=1

Picture Gallery 8
*Hommage à Nelligan* painting
partie de la collection de l'Université de Montréal
https://quartierlibre.ca/art-sur-le-campus-beaute-inaccessible/

# Bibliography

Alharbi, Sarah, « La migration du symbolisme parisien au Canada français et sa réception à l'épreuve du nationalisme: le cas de la poésie d'Émile Nelligan », *Voix Plurielles*, November 2011, available on researchgate.com.

Arella, Suet-Lin, « Rêve d'artiste: la littérature, la musique et l'histoire de l'art dans la poésie d'Émile Nelligan », master's thesis, Université de Montréal, Sept 2019, available at papyrus.bib.umontreal.ca.

Bataïni, Marie Thérèse, *Trois poètes québécois*, XYZ éditeur, Montréal, 2007.

Beausoleil, Claude, « Émile Nelligan et le temps », *Nuit blanche #74* , 1999, available on erudit.org.

Bennett, Paul, « Nelligan est-il l'auteur de ses vers », ledevoir.com, 7 décembre 2013.

Bertrand, Réal, *Émile Nelligan*, Lidec, Montréal, 1980.

Blais, Jacques, « Décadence chez Nelligan: le cas du poème « [Je veux m'éluder] », *Poésie québécoise et histoire littéraire,* hiver 1999.

Brault, Gerard J., *The French Canadian Heritage in New England,* McGill-Queen's University Press, Kingston, Ont., 1986.

Brissette, Pascal, « Le poète qui récitait des vers par-delà le tombeau », *Voix et Images,* Vol 36 # 3, Printemps-Été 2011. Includes information on Nelligan's asylum years.

Chamberland, Roger, « Nelligan livré aux fauves de l'interprétation », *Voix et Images*, printemps 1993.

Chevalier, Jean and Gheerbrant, Alain, *Dictionnaire des symboles*, Robert Laffont / Jupiter, Paris, 1982.

Cogswell, Fred, ed. and trans., *The Complete Poems of Emile Nelligan*, Harvest House, Montréal, 1983.

Cohen, Henry, « Le Rondel dans la poésie d'Émile Nelligan », journals.hil.unb.ca, April 2014.

Courteau, Bernard, *Émile Nelligan, Journal intime,* Guérin, Montréal, 2012.

Courteau, Bernard, *Nelligan n'était pas fou!,* Louise Courteau éditrice, Montréal, 1986.

Couture, François and Rajotte, Pierre, « L'École littéraire de Montréal et ses mythes », *Études françaises*, Vol 36 #3, 2000, on erudit.org.

Dantin, Louis, *Émile Nelligan et son Œuvre* [1904], édition critique par Réjean Robidoux, Les Presses de l'Université de Montréal, 1997. (*Nell. Œuvre*)

Di Saverio, Marc, *The Ship of Gold: The Essential Poems of Émile Nelligan*, Signal Editions, Montréal, 2017.

Doucet, Sophie, « Robertine Barry (1863-1910) », lecture sponsored by la Fondation Lionel-Groulx, Montréal, November 5, 2019.

Francoli, Yvette, *Le Naufragé du Vaisseau d'or, Les vies secrètes de Louis Dantin*, Del Busso Éditeur, Montréal, 2013.

Garon, Yves, ed., *Louis Dantin*, Éditions Fides, Montréal, 1968.

Gill, Charles, « Émile Nelligan », *Le Nationaliste*, March 6, 1904, Bibliothèque et Archives nationales du Québec.

Hayward, Annette and Vandendorpe, Christian, « Dantin et Nelligan au piège de la fiction: Le Naufragé du vaisseau d'or d'Yvette Francoli », *Analyses, revue des littératures franco-canadiennes et québécoise*, vol. 11, no. 2, printemps-été 2016, available at uottawa.scholarsportal.

Hirsch, Edward, *A Poet's Glossary*, Houghton Mifflin Harcourt, Boston, 2014.

Lacourcière, Luc, *Poésies Complètes*, Éditions Fides, Montréal, 1952. First compilation of the entirety of Nelligan's pre-asylum work.

Lemaire, Michel, « Quelques poèmes retrouvés d'Albert Lozeau », *Liberté*, août 1998.

Lemieux, Pierre, *Nelligan amoureux*, Éditions Fides, 1991. (*Nell. am.*)

Marcotte, Hélène, review of *Ces beaux gars à l'œil brun dont rêvait Nelligan* by Bernard Courteau, *University of Toronto Quarterly*, vol. 82, no. 3, Summer 2013.

Michon, Jacques, « Émile Nelligan entre les mots et les choses, poèmes et textes d'asile », *Voix et Images*, printemps 1993, on erudit.org.

Michon, Jacques and Gervais, André, eds., *Poèmes et Textes d'Asile*, Éditions Fides, 1991. Includes the written material that survives from Nelligan's asylum years.

Nantais, Aude and Tremblay, Jean-Joseph, *Portrait de Nelligan déchiré*, Éditions de l'Hexagone, Montréal, 1992.

Nazaruk, Maja, « Émile Nelligan, un Dante d'une époque déchue », *Montreal Review*, Avril, 2013.

Nelligan, Émile, *Poésies complètes 1896-1899*, La Bibliothèque électronique du Québec, Collection Littérature québécoise, Vol. 43: version 2.01.

Nobell, Natasha, « Nelligan, Neige noire et 'la nouvelle Norvège': une mélancolie nordique », archipel.uqam.ca, 2008.

Robidoux, Réjean and Wyczynski, Paul, Émile Nelligan, *Poésies Complètes, 1896-1941*, Bibliothèque québécoise, 1992.

Robidoux, Réjean, « Nelligan n'était pas fou, il acceptait seulement de passer pour ce fou qui s'appelait Nelligan », *Lettres québécoises*, Numéro 44, hiver 1986-1987. A review of Bernard Courteau's *Nelligan n'était pas fou!*

Smith, A.J.M., "Symbolism in Poetry", *McGill Fortnightly Review*, Vol. 1, #2, Dec 5, 1925.

Talbot, Emile, *Reading Nelligan*, McGill-Queen's University Press, Montréal, 2002. (*Reading Nell.*)

Tremblay, Michel, *Nelligan*, Leméac éditeur, Ottawa, 1990.

Vanasse, André, *Émile Nelligan. Le spasme de vivre*, XYZ éditeurs, Montréal, 1996. A novelization. (*Nell. spasme*)

Wyczynski, Paul, *Album Nelligan*, Éditions Fides, 2002. A hefty assemblage of photographs concerning Nelligan, his family and friends, his world and his work. (*Alb. Nell.*)

Wyczynski, Paul, *Nelligan 1879-1941 Biographie*, Éditions Fides, Montréal, 1987. (*Nell. Bio.*)

Wyczynski, Paul, « Nelligan devant la critique », *Québec français*, March 1977.